ENRAPTURED SPACE

ENRAPTURED SPACE

Gender, Class, and Ecology in the Work of Paula Meehan

KATHRYN J. KIRKPATRICK

WEST VIRGINIA UNIVERSITY PRESS

MORGANTOWN

Library of Congress Cataloging-in-Publication Data
Names: Kirkpatrick, Kathryn J., author.
Title: Enraptured space : gender, class, and ecology in the
work of Paula Meehan / Kathryn Kirkpatrick.
Description: First edition. | Morgantown : West Virginia University Press,
2025. | Includes bibliographical references.
Identifiers: LCCN 2024038413 | ISBN 9781959000457 (paperback)
| ISBN 9781959000464 (ebook)
Subjects: LCSH: Meehan, Paula—Criticism and interpretation. | English
poetry—Irish authors—History and criticism. | English poetry—Women
authors—History and criticism. | Irish poetry—Women authors—History
and criticism.
Classification: LCC PR6063.E34 Z75 2025 | DDC 821/.92—dc23/
eng/20250121
LC record available at https://lccn.loc.gov/2024038413

For EU safety/GPSR concerns, please direct inquiries to
WVUPress@mail.wvu.edu or our physical mailing address at
West Virginia University Press / PO Box 6295 / West Virginia University
Morgantown, WV, 26508, USA.

Cover and book design by Than Saffel
Cover image courtesy of Marc O'Sullivan

For we use the myths as mirrors, as we use dreams,
as we use poems.

—*Paula Meehan*

CONTENTS

———

Acknowledgments   ix

Introduction
In Medias Res   1

Chapter 1
Witnessing Class Trauma   20

Chapter 2
Resisting Environmental Injustice   47

Chapter 3
Toward an Animistic Vision   72

Chapter 4
Restoring the Garden   88

Chapter 5
Beyond Human Exceptionalism   114

Chapter 6
The Shamanic Poet   143

Afterword   169

Works Cited   173
Index   181

ACKNOWLEDGMENTS

———

My thanks to Derek Krissoff, whose innovative lists at West Virginia University Press drew me and whose support for this hybrid academic project continued even after he took up new work. Than Saffel, Marguerite Avery, Kristen Bettcher, and Natalie Homer have all supplied invaluable guidance as I've made my way through the publication process. University research grants from Appalachian State funded more than one trip to Ireland.

I acknowledge with deep gratitude my Irish studies friends and colleagues, whose warm support over decades of conferences, conversations, and friendship have helped sustain this project, including Nathalie Anderson, Christine Cusick, Joseph Lennon, Ed Madden, Maureen O'Connor, Drucilla Wall, and Eamonn Wall. At critical points Molly Peacock helped me to have the courage of my vision; her kindness and brilliant example have been crucial.

This book draws on my thinking and writing across twenty years and more. I am thankful for every publisher and editor I contacted who has graciously granted permission for including revised versions of previously published material. Chapter 1 revises and expands on "'Between Breath and No Breath': Witnessing Class Trauma in Paula Meehan's *Dharmakaya*," in *An Sionnach: A Journal of Literature, Arts, and Culture*, vol. 1, no. 2, fall 2005. The same is true of chapter 2 and "Between Country and City: Paula Meehan's Ecofeminist Poetics," in *Murmurs that Come Out of the Earth: Eco-critical Readings of Irish Texts,* edited by Christine

Cusick (U of Cork P, 2010). Chapter 3 revisits "A Murmuration of Starlings in the Rowan Tree: Finding Gary Snyder in the Work of Paula Meehan" in the special issue on Paula Meehan, edited by Jody Allen Randolph, of *An Sionnach: A Journal of Literature, Arts, and Culture*, vol. 5, nos. 1 & 2, spring/fall 2009. Chapter 4 appeared earlier as "Paula Meehan's Gardens" in *New Hibernia Review*, vol. 17, no. 2, summer 2013. Chapter 5 includes a section of "Animals and Climate Crisis in Irish Poetry" in *The Cambridge History of Literature and The Environment,* edited by Malcom Sen (Cambridge UP, 2022), and Chapter 6 incorporates elements of "Memory in Paula Meehan's *Geomantics*," in *Irish University Review*, vol. 47, no. 1, spring 2017, as well as a section of "Paula Meehan and the Public Poem" in *Cambridge History of Irish Women's Poetry*, edited by Ailbhe Darcy and David Wheatley (Cambridge UP, 2021).

I have quoted from the following collections by Paula Meehan:

- *Dharmakaya (D)*, Carnanet Press, 2000
- *The Man Who Was Marked by Winter (MMW)*, Gallery Press, 1991
- *Painting Rain (PR)*, Carcanet, 2009
- *Pillow Talk (PT)*, Gallery Press, 1994
- *Reading the Sky (RS),* Beaver Row Press, 1986
- *Return and No Blame (RNB)*, Beaver Row Press, 1984

Like a shirt worn inside out, this book weaves into itself the process of its own making. What began as a felt connection with Paula Meehan's poems later became a path toward another kind of academic writing. *Enraptured Space* would not exist, certainly not in its present form, without the wisdom, goodwill, and kindness of Paula Meehan herself. She has graciously answered questions, engaged in broad-ranging conversations, and offered hospitalities large and small. I have been transformed as a poet and a scholar by her work.

And, finally, enduring love and thanks to Will Atkinson, with me every step of the way.

Introduction

IN MEDIAS RES

———

Over twenty years ago, R. T. Smith, the longtime editor of *Shenandoah* literary journal, asked me to review a new book of poetry by an Irish poet whose work I didn't know well. I was at the time focusing my scholarly energies on the prose of nineteenth-century Irish women writers while also scratching out time for my own poetry. Paula Meehan's Carcanet edition of *Dharmakaya* (2000) arrived in my life as a powerful suggestion. Meehan herself describes the book as a "gear shift," the poetic project of the earlier work accelerated and intensified. For me it was a lane change. Stretched by a heavy teaching load and long hours in archives, I had less and less time for the poetry practice that sustained me. *Dharmakaya* modeled a synthesis I hadn't yet made between witness and craft, gender and class, ecology and agency. I came away from those poems regrounded. Audre Lorde famously observed, "Poetry is not a luxury." Meehan has made the case even more directly: "I believe that two lines of poetry can save a life" (Hayden).

Changing lanes meant making more time for the writing of poetry and shifting my scholarly focus to contemporary Irish poetry in general and Meehan's work in particular. I knew I could learn from Meehan as a poet because her mastery of craft was clear. Like many Irish poets, she is at home in the sonnet, the villanelle, and other forms, as well as in free verse. But beyond that, I found in her work a complex and moving exploration of the vicissitudes of growing up working class. Meehan's poems quite literally *see* what many poems do not: the diminishing effects of neoliberal capitalist culture on working-class individuals and communities as well as the larger multispecies worlds of which we are all a part. By refusing as "natural" the class structure and social realities created by an extractive economic system, Meehan's work also charts the ways elements of a premodern animistic vision might be retrieved in order to rewrite modernity's catastrophic legacy for life on earth in the twenty-first century.

I was prepared to see the contribution of Meehan's work because I was parented by a mother and father who had navigated poverty in their own childhoods and whose class trauma formed the context in which I was raised. The son of an itinerant pipe fitter, my father had joined the Air Force and scrabbled with my mother the nomadic lower-middle-class life of my childhood, which often felt lived in the margins of an affluent U.S. culture. It wasn't until I read the working-class critic Raymond Williams and Karl Marx himself that I began to see how a conditioned and internalized class degradation could be demystified and reframed. I found in Meehan's poems a perspective I recognized as hard-won, a poetic voice strong enough to revalue and reclaim lives that the dominant culture had disregarded. That has been an incalculable good in my own life and in the lives of other readers. One goal of this book is to ensure that the project of Meehan's work is even more broadly known and appreciated. In our current era of economic, social, and environmental upheaval, her poems are, in Seamus Heaney's terms, "strong enough to help" (Heaney, *Redress* 9).

* * *

In an interview with Jody Allen Randolph at University College Dublin just before the release of Meehan's collection *Geomantic* (2016), Meehan observed that literary critics are often unaware of how much of themselves they reveal in their own writing: "Poems are like mirrors. People look into them and the poem is reading them, their education, their vocabulary, their emotional tenor; it reads what they bring to it" (Allen Randolph, "Conversation"). This book is also a record of the ways that Meehan's poems have read and continue to read me. When she learned that as well as a literary scholar I am also a practicing poet, engaged with issues of prosody and craft as a maker of poems, Meehan told me she understood better why I had been able to enter the world of her poems so fully. With seven published collections of my own poems, I bring to this project a double engagement with poetic craft and scholarly methods.

Our practices are transformative; we make and remake ourselves through the lives we live and what we make of them. I want to bring to literary criticism more of what I experience as a writer of poetry: an ancient genre where the experience of mystery, imagination, and transformation is made and shared, poetry can enact powerful re-engagements with a living earth in part because the process of making a poem—through its dance of line, syntax, image, sound, and sense—pitches the poet into a remarkably enchanted realm. No poet can deny for long the presence within the self of knowledge beyond what one consciously knows nor of an agency beyond the individual personality. Seamus Heaney once described the poems in his volume *Seeing Things* as inspired by something that wanted to be voiced. This book explores such reciprocal relationships between the poet and a living, responding world.

* * *

A central figure in my nomadic childhood was a sycamore I helped my father plant, which grew beyond all imagining and despite frequent pruning in the front yard of the small brick house where he spent his last years. That sycamore still grows in the yard of my former childhood home as if it means to live the 400 years sycamores as a species are heir to, if not often granted. The Carcanet edition of Paula Meehan's *Dharmakaya* features a cover photograph by Ita Kelly of an enormous, gnarled sycamore, its several amputated branches healed over beneath a still thriving canopy, a gathering of picked flowers offered at its base. Entitled "Evidence of Tree Worship in the Botanic Gardens," the photograph and its title manage to evoke both modernity's scientific gaze and a premodern belief in the animate spirits of trees. Inspired by Meehan's work and vision, I want to evoke these ranges of knowing here. Indeed, *Dharmakaya*'s cover image brought me enormous joy when I confirmed the identity of that tree through Meehan herself. It has led me to propose that her work engages in a "strategic animism" whereby a knowing subject enacts re-engagements with efficacious belief systems from the past. But poets, of course, have always embraced knowing in more than one way. The poet in me knows that the giant sycamore still living in the yard of my former childhood home resonates with *Dharmakaya*'s cover, which found me at a time when I needed and wanted to make a turning.

While writing about the trees I found in Meehan's poems, I walked on my own ridge in the Blue Ridge Mountains of North Carolina and glimpsed in a series of uncanny moments one afternoon those enormous red oaks and sugar maples as animate beings. The woods felt enchanted, and I walked with a sublime awe both exhilarating and terrifying. That was not a feeling that would ever have allowed logging, and I have the good fortune to intend that land and those trees for the protection of a land trust.

As Sharae Deckard observes, literary and cultural representations play a role in supporting the whole web of life in Ireland and beyond by offering "alternative conceptions of value that repudiate capitalism's devaluing of human and extra-human life" (41). From her now-iconic ecocritical poem "Death of a Field" to "The Solace of Artemis," Meehan's work witnesses to capitalism's devaluing of human and more-than-human life while also repeatedly providing rich alternative visions. In these ways Meehan's work gives readers resources for transforming what it means to be human. Addressing her writing fully requires an expansive ecocritical frame, one that acknowledges the interconnections between exploitative economic systems, social inequities, and environmental degradation. Meehan's work also asks us to move beyond an opposition between "writer" and "activist" toward what postcolonial ecocritics Graham Huggan and Helen Tiffin describe as a perspective "attentive to the negotiations between political imperative and aesthetic play" (33). Similarly, Rob Nixon, in his influential *Slow Violence and the Environmentalism of the Poor*, identifies his subjects, among them Ken Saro-Wiwa, Arundhati Roy, Jamaica Kincaid, and June Jordan, as "writer-activists" who help us recognize the social and environmental violences discounted by dominant structures of apprehension: "Who gets to see, and from where? When and how does such empowered seeing become normative? And what perspectives—not least those of the poor or women or the colonized—do hegemonic sight conventions of visuality obscure?" (15). In *Postcolonial Ecocriticism*, Huggan and Tiffin advocate for "criticism which appreciates the enduring noninstrumentality of environmental writing, as well as gauging its continuing usefulness in mobilising individual and collective support" (33). Activist literary fields have always engaged in the both/ and of aesthetic beauty and social transformation: cultural artifacts that witness powerfully to injustice, as Meehan's poems do, work on the reader's apprehension precisely through the strength of their craft. In this context, the critic's role is, as Nixon suggests, to explore the capacities of a writing of witness to challenge social injustice by committing to a literary and cultural criticism that aims to intervene. Limiting the critic's role to the discussion of poetry as an aesthetic object involves a failure to fully engage with a writer's vision. A dialogue between Meehan's poems and the fields of ecofeminism, environmental justice, postcolonial ecocriticism, class studies, and critical animal studies makes possible a rich elaboration of her work.

The structure of this book is informed by the associational leaps and resonances on which poetry thrives. Anthropologist Susan Lepselter has described *resonance* as

> the intensification produced by the overlapping, back and forth
> call of signs from various discourses. . . . [T]he connections feel
> vertically layered, rather than horizontally bridged. Resonance
> is not an exact iteration. Rather it's something that strikes a
> chord, that inexplicably rings true, a sound whose notes are pro-
> longed. It is just-glimpsed connections and hidden structures
> that are felt to shimmer below the surface of things. (4)

Similarly, this book deals in figures and metaphors in an exploration of multiple ways of making meaning. It includes a series
of broad-ranging micro-interviews with Meehan herself, sometimes focused on poems that I and others have found especially
significant in her work. The interviews are meant to both ground
and unground my own readings, expose the seams and gaps that
literary criticism always contains though often conceals, celebrate
multiplicities of readings, include the maker's significant voice as
one among others, and leave visible the tracks for others to follow
into and out of analysis, collaboration, and dialogue. Poets often
work to capture on the page the process of the transformative
moment or insight. I am working to preserve elements of that
process here, while also honoring the crafting of an interpretive artifact. If we are at the end of a global cultural narrative of
progress and of freedom for some secured by the lives of workers, other creatures, and the living planet, what does it mean to
live and, as writers and scholars, to know and write beyond an
evolutionary cul-de-sac? Anna Lowenhaupt Tsing has suggested
that in these final stages of capitalism, when definitions of progress as material growth have stopped making sense, we might
look around rather than look ahead and embrace the future as
indeterminant and multidirectional (2–9). Meehan's poems participate boldly in the cultural project of envisioning another kind
of world.

I take the title for this book from Meehan's early collection *Pillow Talk*: "One Evening in May" describes a narrator's

encounter with a pagan goddess, who "parted clouds, // revealed her starry body, her great / snakeshead, her myriad children / feasting at her breasts" (*PT* 16). The experience leaves the narrator humbled and changed:

> I thought I was wise
> till I heard her voice; thought
> I had the art of mirror plumbing
> perfected. Then she showed me
>
> in a blue clearing of clouds
> how space can enrapture a mortal.
> That small glimpse was worth
> all the age's talk in the academies. (*PT* 16)

The confident agency of the "I" in this poem gives way to the power of a goddess emissary from the earth. And this reanimation of a living world becomes central to the poet's vocation. To enrapture is to "inspire with overmastering poetic fervor" (*OED*). There's a clever chiming here with "rapture" and the Christian sense of heavenly transport, but neither Meehan's poem nor the overarching trajectory of her work aim to leave solid ground. Instead, the goddess, with "showed me" and "small glimpse," endows the narrator with a second sight, "a daze" that re-enchants her embodied experience *in* the world.

Peter Linebaugh observes that "[t]he word 'enchantment' comes from a French word, 'chanter,' to sing. . . . [I]f we understand 'song' to include poetry, then the call for enchanting the world, for singing creation into being, is both rhapsodic and prophetic. It is a choral accomplishment" (xvii). John Felstiner in *Can Poetry Save the Earth?* describes the poet's practice as an intimate relationship with an animate nature in which the poet's "attention to detail is a species of love" (269). These writers gesture toward reciprocal relationships between the poet and a living, responding world. Peggy Barlett describes re-enchantment thus: "Separate from the rational, but not incompatible with it, this way of knowing involves a sensory, affective engagement that includes dimensions of wonder and delight and embraces an identity that includes connections to other species and the earth's living systems" (1077). Silvia Federici contextualizes the project of re-enchantment as a challenge to the world system of global capitalism: "By 'disenchantment' [Max] Weber referred to the vanishing of the religious and the sacred from the world. But we can interpret his warning in a more political sense, as referring to the emergence of a world in which our capacity to recognize the existence of a logic other than that of capitalist development is every day more in question" (*Re-enchanting* 188). Although Meehan makes visible the desperation of working-class lives and a wounded natural world in a decolonized Ireland recolonized by global capitalism, her work offers profound alternative visions. As an "urban" poet writing from the location of working-class woman, Meehan's work retrieves elements of precolonial imaginative worldviews, representing nature as unappropriable other. This acknowledgment of and respect for otherness enacts a re-enchantment of the natural world and becomes a way of naming a fundamental wilderness in the self.

* * *

My understanding of class in the context of literary studies was formed by my engagement with the work of Raymond Williams, whose landmark book *The Country and the City* reread the English literary canon from a working-class perspective, asking important questions about how literary representations, as for instance in Ben Johnson's poem *To Penshurst,* colluded in mystifications of who did the labor and provided the plenty for the landed estate (27–31). Williams taught me that literature does class-bound cultural work and the worlds that writers create through language are not neutral portrayals of power relations. Nor is the social construction of values in literature timeless and transcendent. Williams's *Marxism and Literature* explores the complex imbrications of class location and literary representation and, along with the work of Terry Eagleton and Stuart Hall, establishes the powerful methodologies and perspectives of cultural studies that inform the writing of so many scholars, including those in the environmental humanities.

The kind of witness to interior life that a poetry like Meehan's performs provides valuable contributions to a more open-ended study of class described by J. K. Gibson-Graham, Stephen Resnick, and Richard Wolff as the study of "economic difference." These class studies scholars suggest that perspectives from various class locations or "a heterogenously classed landscape" can offer "hitherto unglimpsed opportunities for projects of change" (14): "Given the different types of class relations, the different moments of the class process, and the different relations of class to other dimensions of identity, narrative and emotional possibilities are infinite" (16). Meehan has been variously described as a citizen poet and a vocational poet. Her own class position has shifted, and as Nicholas Grene suggests, the term "working-class," if used alone, could as easily reduce her writing as amplify it. Labor historian David Roediger argues that scholars are bound to "the simultaneous consideration of multiple social identities and social positions such as those of class, gender, and race. . . . Such multiplicity does not make class even a modicum less important, but it does relocate class within an ensemble of social relations, identities, and dreams" (34). Roediger directs class studies to the rich reservoir of witness in poetry by writers raised in and/or living in working-class cultures. Engaging with such poetry becomes one way of moving beyond reductive or incidental considerations of class toward an understanding of the broader perceptual framings the lived experience of social class produces. Just so, Meehan's poems demonstrate how significant a working-class subject location can be for what a poet is able to *see*.

As Friedrich Engels documented well in *The Condition of the Working Class in England*, bourgeois culture is often so arranged that, quite literally, through a spatial lack of proximity, it is possible to render invisible the oppressive conditions in which poor communities live and work. Moreover, Marx's great insight was that capitalist economies rely on the extraction of labor from the working-class communities they impoverish through the mechanisms of surplus labor and value, which continually squeeze wages at or below subsistence. Having lived these conditions herself, Meehan exposes in her poems the exploitative class structures that enable bourgeois and upper-class affluence. Her poems witness to those who not only fail to benefit from modernity's reliance on an exploitative economy but who inevitably suffer the class trauma produced by such economic and social relations. Indeed, the degraded terms on which systems of cultural dominance rely—woman, working class, animal—are reclaimed and revalued in her poems. I suggest that Meehan does this cultural work in part through her representation of space. In many of her poems, the boundaries between public and private, outside and inside, are intimately informed by a subject location that does not accept bourgeois categories as "natural." As boundary crosser between the human and animal, the material and supernatural, the shape-shifter is an apt emblem for a poet whose working-class vision exposes a dominant culture's categories as constructed.

* * *

The chapters here follow my own unfolding exploration of Meehan's poems. I've titled this introduction "In Medias Res" because *Dharmakaya* was a midcareer breakthrough for Meehan and, as it turns out, for me. I explore the elements of this "gear change" in *Dharmakaya* in the following chapter. That collection of poetry inspired not only a shift of my scholarly focus but also something new in my poems: Meehan's work made my own poems braver and stronger. Once I had engaged with *Dharmakaya*, I wanted to understand more about how Meehan had arrived at such powerfully poised poems of witness. In chapter 2, I visit the volumes preceding *Dharmakaya* and which, to my mind, prepare the way for it. Chapter 3 traces a trope, the garden, which I find significant for the concerns of the preceding chapters, especially a developing animism in Meehan's work. In chapter 4, I circle back around to one of Meehan's most formative and enduring influences, the work of her mentor, U.S. poet Gary Snyder. Chapter 5 explores, through a critical ecofeminist lens, Meehan's innovative, shape-shifting essays, first given as lectures during her Ireland Professor of Poetry tenure (2013–2015). This study lands in chapter 6 with a reading of Meehan's poems, particularly those in *Painting Rain* (2009) and *Geomantic* (2016), as the work of a late modern shamanic poet, a role that includes another of her unique contributions to Irish and world poetry, her development of the public poem in Ireland.

INTERVIEW

....

THE SELF ON THE LINE, 2019

KATHRYN KIRKPATRICK: I'm interested in what you're thinking about poetry as a hybrid form, and I'm also drawn to scholarship that's evolving into more hybrid forms.

PAULA MEEHAN: It may be that there will be, already is, some branch of poetry that is a hybrid with scholarship. A great deal of poetry, some contemporary collections of the last few years, certainly seem to have a desire to focus on the etymology of the very words that they're using—an almost in-built critique of the process itself, or an extended explanation of the process. Other strategies include a merging of public with private history, or the use of metadata, a kind of play now with AI [artificial intelligence].

KK: What I see in scholarship is the more associative logic. It's especially happening with anthropologists. They were early on the scene, always including their own experiences as observers. And I'm also responding to feminists, who, all the way back to Virginia Woolf, were emphasizing the lived life behind the "I" in anything that was written. People are talking about "braided narratives" as well. But it's more that the logic is not so forced into this kind of . . . causation.

PM: It's a more holistic way of gathering knowledge, interpreting it, and transmitting it. Poetry has always excelled at braiding knowledge: Gary Snyder says we are top of the food chain— we use others' research in various fields of scholarship all the time in our work.

KK: Yes. And were you intending something like that when you were writing the Ireland Professor of Poetry lectures?

PM: Oh, completely, because I'm not, in the narrow sense of the word, an academic. My primary response to text, or to anything, is not an academic one, you know. My desire is always for embodiment. If I can't dance it, the poem, I can lose interest very fast. But I do watch those movements in criticism, because they're part of the phenomenology of the world, and they also directly impact on my living. I've been labeled in many ways, looked at through many lenses. Urban poet, working-class poet, woman poet, feminist poet, republican poet, with a small r, Catholic poet, with a capital C, Buddhist poet. Ecopoet! For me, as a maker and a craftswoman, in the flux of making, there is only one lens. Poet—good or bad. The most interesting critique and engagement, for me, is always the conversation between peers. Or between student and teacher. What happens in the moment in a workshop. That's a really fascinating conversation from both ends.

I have real problems with the academic training in the West. I don't know enough about other places. I mean, I could see how you could have a critique about other traditions, like the Buddhist tradition; they are every bit as open to the hierarchical abuse of power as the Catholics or any institution, whether it is in the university or the prison. You know, the institutionalized mind seeks to calibrate in a hierarchical way. It is such a dead end in philosophy and in all of the arts and the humanities. I'm more interested in the kind of witness that puts the self on the line and engages with the whole person, with their class allegiance, with their own souls as well as their brains.

KK: One of the things that has sometimes troubled me as a poet is that there can be quite a big separation between "creative writers," for lack of a better word, and scholars. I have tried to do both, and I feel like that kind of interweaving has been really helpful. I like having an omnivorous mind. I do feel like that is a writerly orientation.

PM: One of the roots of my own interest in a cross-discipline approach was Gary Snyder's undergraduate thesis at Reed College, "He Who Hunted Birds in His Father's Village: The

Dimensions of a Haida Myth." It looked at a Haida myth through many lenses—anthropological, linguistic, historical, naturalist, etc., a multifaceted lens, diamond sharp. It was revolutionary. Or maybe it's just a moment of revolution that I tuned into. I'm sure other people were doing it because I don't think he's a singular iteration. I think he's an iteration of the beginning of a global consciousness through those fifty strange years with satellites and Sputniks that allowed us the eyes to see the earth whole. Snyder was an early direction finder for my practice as a poet. So that thesis is very important to me, and it did give a model for how the academy could actually be more holistic and fluid and creative. It was a real signpost.

To put in the balance against that, when I spoke about having a multidisciplinary approach to Irish poetry at a conference at Notre Dame [University], around 2012, I met quite a bit of resistance. I was surprised by an historian who felt very threatened that an anthropologist or a poet might just stumble in there into his area, history. That undergraduate thesis of Snyder's was written in the 1950s, and now we're more than half a century farther along, and you can still see resistance. A kind of siloing of knowledge systems.

KK: You know, I got an interdisciplinary PhD, and the training was around the care that a scholar uses with documents. That was all very welcome. You started with an issue, a really burning question, and then you went everywhere to look into it. You didn't just stay in one place, one discipline. J. M. Coetzee, the South African, he's just so brilliant in his multidisciplinary approach to writing. I think that that kind of depth (and I see it so much in your work, too), a broad reading, a real study, a passion-directed study, comes through in the writing, and the work is not *only* a focus on craft. Perhaps no one only focuses on craft, but there are times when I feel like the craft in a poem is quite beautiful, but I'm not very interested in what's being said.

PM: Well, it's what the lyric is always vulnerable to—ornamentation. We inherit such highly ornamented and coded linguistic models, especially with received forms, those lovely patterns handed down through the ages. They are quite seductive, especially on the ear. But the danger is you might end up writing to and for an audience that is dead, if you write the nineteenth-century literary ballad, say, or the sixteenth-century sonnet. But I believe somewhere inside me is a modernist who wants form to follow function, in a cold and stripped-down way. I love the making, I love the play involved in upcycling or reinhabiting the received forms, but I need to have more than just a good playtime to publish them. Do you know what I mean? To offer them out to some imagined community, they have to be *more than* somehow—or do they? That's a question. Do they?

KK: Can we then talk about "The Exact Moment I Became a Poet"? I think of that poem as one of a series of ars poeticas in your work, this one articulated midcareer. What is your relationship with that poem now, and do you think ars poetica is an accurate way to think about it?

PM: Your relationship with poems will change, as you know. And, in fact, one of the questions I was going to ask you was, did you find, when you were taking your poems around with you, did you find out, in the middle maybe of reading them, "Jesus, that's what I meant"? Because they also reveal themselves to the maker over time. And you start to understand actually what you were at and what you were doing, though you may have just groped it out when you were making the poem.

KK: Yes, and that feels like part of the magic of poems to me.

PM: Well, that poem ["The Exact Moment I Became a Poet"] is dedicated to Kay Foran, who had the same teacher as me back in primary school, the Central Model Girls' School, Miss Shannon. We weren't in the same class, but she had the same teacher. So Kay grew up in my old neighborhood, and she's a marvelous person. She became one of the great literacy teachers of the north inner city, involved in the Dublin Adult Learning Centre. She retired a couple of years ago, but writes, always writes, a lot of memoir-based pieces. She can recreate our old neighborhood, remember it, repopulate it, and one of the joys of my life is shooting the breeze with her. I go to her to check my own memory against her memory. Does that make sense?

KK: Yes, of course.

PM: I say, "Do you remember the suits Miss Shannon wore?" She had two suits which she switched week on week, and they would've been bouclé knits—fine, fine wool. Probably machine knit and hand finished, a navy one and a brown one. And the skirt was knit, they were all knitted, but the skirt was given the appearance of pleats by the way they were knitted with stocking stitch and purls in between. Not gathered but giving an impression of gathered. I remember so distinctly everything about her, but I do have to check with Kay about some things about the old days. She is a very, very good friend, and we discovered each other well after we had both left school. I discovered her through working in the same projects that she was involved in, mostly second-chance education in the north inner city. So the poem is dedicated to her, with all this realization of her.

KK: She [Miss Shannon] would have been someone who was having her clothes made by these factory workers, right? You have your own clothes being made at home, and then there's the teacher in the poem telling you to be careful or you'll end up in the sewing factory. And you're recalling her clothes which had been made by some of these women who were related to you?

PM: I don't know where Miss Shannon had her clothes made, or where she bought them. And my sisters were all younger than me, but later when they left school they would have worked in the sewing factories. But some neighbors and one of my aunts were working in the sweatshops during the time in which the poem is set. The culture of the sewing factories was very familiar—many of the girls left school at fourteen, the legal age to leave school at the time, the legal age to marry, too, as it happened. One of my sisters is still a seamstress, with her own thriving business. Those days there were still sewing apprenticeships because, you know, there was still a clothing industry in Dublin, so many of my schoolmates went into the sweatshops. But they would have gotten their seven years' apprenticeship. Now my mother was gifted with her hands; she never trained formally in dressmaking, but she taught me many of those feminine arts, as they would have been considered then—sewing, crochet, embroidery, smocking, knitting, I would have had a very intense training in all of them, at my mother's knee and at my grandmother Mary's knee. Most of what we wore was homemade or hand-me-downs. Ironically, we were being prepared in primary school for a world that was ending. All the traditional industries of the city, the sustaining jobs for holding city communities together, were heading toward redundancy. I saw the factories right at the moment of stability before cheap Chinese imports took over. And that was the end of so many lives as factory girls or workers.

The work of hands fascinates me, but also Miss Shannon was right, you know. The only way out of that life, of poor pay and exploitation, was and is, to this very day, an education. She taught us the rudiments of Latin and French—the handful of us whom she perceived as bright—those of us she thought might go to secondary school. There were maybe three of us, you know, who actually went. It was, and I knew it at the time, a very reductive idea of brightness! So the complex of energies from the community and the culture, they just interest me and will continue always to interest me.

KK: It's as if you're drawing this poem, which I've called an ars poetica, you're drawing it as a communal project. Do you know what I mean? By talking about all the ways that Kay was involved and all the ways you're verifying all the details, it's like the composition of it depends on the community, right?

PM: Yes, totally. I mean it depends also on an imagined community, who sit like judges, they sit in judgment. It's not always a comfortable thing. Actually, I'll say it's not a comfortable thing, but they are my imagined elective consistory against which I measure certain things, not everything. But for certain kinds of poetry or poems on certain subjects, I hold the community where I grew up, where I got language, as a kind of jury I stand before. Kay was definitely the forewoman of the jury I stood before when I wrote that poem. And, curiously, for it's a synchronicity, Kay often buys me clothes!

KK: Oh, nice!

PM: Yeah! She'd be around the vintage and the charity shops, and she'd see something she thinks might suit me, and it very often does. I go round those shops too. I'm a hoker in bins of old embroideries. I especially value anything made by hand—probably because as a child I didn't value my mother's wonderful handiwork enough.

KK: That's really sweet.

PM: I got the end of a Victorian education; we were being prepared mostly for a life in service, or maybe in a shop, but certainly in the factories, and then to be good Catholic mothers, to stop working after marriage and become good Catholic mothers. I've been back to the Model Schools recently. It's a multicultural, very diverse, co-ed primary school now—it's a fantastic place. There are up to thirty first languages in the school community, and it is very much a reflection of Dublin in the present day. I suppose there's a question, and you'd know it, too, of how much pressure we feel to be some kind of an archivist of community experience as well.

1

WITNESSING CLASS TRAUMA

———

In her 1994 collection *Pillow Talk*, Paula Meehan presents an allegory of class conflict in "She-Who-Walks-Among-The-People." The poem is narrated by a wise woman familiar in Meehan's poems, Granny, whose access to myth and the spirit world gives her utterances the quality of oracle:

> Long, long ago, not in my granny's time,
> nor in her granny's time before her, but further back
> in a world you couldn't imagine, a bad spell
> was cast on the whole island. The people lived
> in fear and pain. The land itself was hurting,
> as were the animals who shared it with the people.
> One tribe fought against the next tribe
> and at night their dreams were muddy and grey.
> One tribe had many, many tokens
> and owned all the land and chariots and most
> of the things on the island. Another tribe
> had some tokens, just enough for food and shelter.
> And some tribes had no tokens at all. None
> of them could get any peace or clear dreamings
> with the worry about tokens, whether they had
> any or not. The tribes who had nothing were
> broken in spirit. Nobody cared about them,

> and nobody listened to them. A terrible silence
> stole over them: words were stones on their tongues. (*PT* 60)

Granny goes on to describe the appearance of a woman from the Northwest, whose "heart opened / with pity for the people and pity for the women / in special." This woman warrior uses her "marvellous gift of speech" to advocate for the silent and in doing so breaks the spell that had kept the people from speaking for themselves. The poem concludes with Granny's remonstrance that her young listener "work hard at your books, / in case one day you'll be needed by the people" (*PT* 60).

This poem's evocation of oppressive class and gender relations, the inseparability of humans from the nonhuman world, the social responsibility of the poet, the pagan as a resource for female agency, and the healing power of compassionate and courageous speech are all central to Meehan's poetics. "I believe that you fight the battles around you as a citizen and that will affect your work" (Praga 75), Meehan has observed of the relationship between her poetry and her socialist-inspired activism and community work. Though she maintains that the poet's "first responsibility is to make good poems" (Praga 73) and delights in poems resilient enough to sustain multiple readings, Meehan's aesthetics are informed by the political and ethical concerns she lives with; as she said in an interview appearing in *Colby Quarterly* in 1992, "I still have trouble thinking of poetry as a career. A poet's training is the life" (Dorgan 268). Raised in a Dublin inner-city community among "what used to be the working class, " Meehan has watched that community change: "we don't have a working class anymore, we have a dispossessed class who have no job and very little hope" (Praga 77). Here she identifies the shift from working-class communities to the fragmented underclass of postindustrialism, those whom cultural theorist Stuart Hall has called the "new poor . . . left behind on every significant dimension of social opportunity" ("New Times" 225). Calling herself a "cultural worker," Meehan observes of her poetic practice: "I'm coming from a perspective where poetry is a political act, an act of resistance, an act of survival" (O'Halloran and Maloy 7). And that act, for Meehan, is never an entirely solitary one or entirely in the service of the self alone. In this way she works to reconnect the poet to an older communal role:

> Poetry in the twentieth century and in the opening of the twenty-first century, in the traditions I've worked in, is chiefly concerned with private memory—a holding up against the mass totalitarian-type states we live in now of the witness of a single human life. I want to push at the border—to try to reconnect with the idea of the poet as holder of public memory, community memory, tribal memory, which has been our job for most of the possibly 40,000 years we've had poetry as a tool of culture. My family poems are the work of a private memorialist with an impulse to express collective memory. (Allen Randolph, *Close to the Next Moment* 27–28)

The project Meehan articulates here use the difference of her class experience to restore a communal role for poetry. Speaking intentionally from a location outside bourgeois privilege, Meehan's poems thus work to make familiar to readers a class subjectivity that may be quite different from their own. This difference appears from the beginning in poems with narrators who challenge a central assumption of both liberal and conservative ideologies: that private life is somehow separate from the political struggles and power relations of the public world. Lacking the insulation provided by economic wealth, Meehan's narrators cannot retreat to domestic spaces protected from class violence. In the opening sequence of her first book, *Return and No Blame* (1984), the speaker stands hidden behind "patched curtains," the poverty of domestic interiors in her old neighborhood—"the abandoned kitchens, the forsaken hallways"—clearly linked to the "gaudy bishops" and politicians processing in the street outside. Adopting the pose of a sniper stalking the city's powerful elite, Meehan here opens her oeuvre with a poem announcing her status as class outlaw with a lived relationship to the public world of the city street; indeed, the narrators in Meehan's poems are more likely to appear outside— in streets or gardens—than in the domestic spaces traditionally prescribed for middle-class women. Later in the volume, "The Apprentice" makes explicit that "a city slum child" cannot learn from a bourgeois poetry tradition where Yeats is master: "The poor become clowns / In your private review", this narrator observes, appropriating Yeats's images for her own purposes. "You are no master of mine. . . . Masters, all bastards" (*RNB* 27). Refusing to separate the political, the ethical, and the aesthetic, Meehan here announces that the difference of her class experience must lead her to her own poetics. Indeed, Eric Falci has argued that even at the level of the micro-structures of Meehan's poems, social justice concerns appear: her "variable stanzas, and the lyric positionings that occur within them, themselves evince an abiding interest in relationality and, more specifically, in the social" (237).

This poetics found especially powerful expression in Meehan's midcareer volume, *Dharmakaya* (2000). Her sixth collection, following the selected poems in *Mysteries of the Home* (1996), *Dharmakaya* frames poems of suffering in urban poverty, turmoil, and longing in familial and sexual relationships, and the strug- gle to resist oppressive definitions of female sexuality and identity with a surprising prescription: Buddhist detachment. In an epi- graph from a commentary on *The Tibetan Book of the Dead*, the reader is reminded of the transitoriness of the temporal world compared with "the experiencer's own consciousness, which has no birth and no death, and is by its very nature immutable light" (*D* 6). The title poem opening the volume echoes this spiritual stance: "become a still pool / in the anarchic flow, the street's / unceasing carnival / of haunted and redeemed." What follows are haunting poems that suggest why a spiritual discipline might be necessary for a poet who has taken as her subject children wit- nessing violence in the home and class violence in the larger soci- ety. Meehan describes the experience of writing these poems as "going into the body's most intimate memories, often below the threshold of what can consciously be recalled, to bring back news to the self. It was a long time in the making and every poem cost me" (O'Halloran and Malory 4). This process of reclaiming links Meehan with the woman in "She-Who-Walks-Among-The-People" whose "heart opened / with pity" for those "who had nothing," the "broken in spirit" afflicted by "a terrible silence" because "[n]obody cared about them, / and nobody listened to them" (*PT* 60). Yet Meehan's inner-city childhood locates her precisely among those for whom nobody cared or listened. By breaking the silence with poems of witness and grieving, Meehan engages in recovery, on both a collective and individual level, from trauma—"the painful aftereffects of a violent history in the body and mind" (Steele 2). In these terms, at midcareer, *Dharmakaya* developed and intensified Meehan's poetic project by invoking a Buddhist spiritual practice in order to witness class trauma.

RECOVERING GRIEVABLE LIVES

Trauma is often described as a particular response to violence: it is not "locatable in the simple violent or original event in an individual's past, but rather in the way that its very unassimilated nature— the way it was precisely *not known* in the first instance—returns to haunt the survivor later on" (Caruth 4). This haunting can manifest itself as a variety of physical and psychic symptoms, including nightmares and flashbacks, which, like the ache of a wound, point to the damage done. Recovery from a traumatic response to violence involves the literal reclaiming of the memories, often in the presence of a sympathetic listener or audience. In *We Heal from Memory*, Cassie Premo Steele describes poetry as a genre uniquely suited for both witnessing to and recovering from violence because "poetry, like trauma, takes images, feelings, rhythms, sounds, and the physical sensations of the body as evidence" (3). By retrieving and reconstructing suffered violence as traces, the poet "transforms 'real experience' into literature through image, metaphor, and re-imagination," and thus "turns the trauma of history into a poetry of witness" (5). Meehan is well aware of the process: "Poetry can be a tool for excavation. . . . Remembering for its own sake wouldn't interest me, but memory as agent for changing the present appeals to me greatly" (O'Halloran and Maloy 13).

While Steele focuses particularly on the work of Anne Sexton, Gloria Anzaldúa, and Audre Lorde, poets who represent race, gender, and sexuality as sites of trauma, Meehan's poetry foregrounds social class; nonetheless, her narrators' experiences of class are often heavily inflected by their sense of themselves as embodied female subjects. In *Keywords* (1976), Raymond Williams observes that a "class is sometimes an economic category, including all who are objectively in that economic situation. But a class is sometimes . . . a formation in which, for historical reasons, consciousness of this situation and the organization to deal with it have developed" (68). Meehan's poems register class in both these senses, charting both material conditions and class consciousness. Her poems witness to the injustices that arise from oppressive economic relations and explore the interior landscapes of individuals living in such contexts, in the process "dealing with" this charged and often painful material by using tools of an emerging spiritual practice. Indeed, the structure of Meehan's *Dharmakaya* suggests that this spiritual practice enables the narrators of these poems to resist the values of a middle-class culture that equates status and worth with position in a class hierarchy.

My use of the term *trauma* when describing the effects of class violence carries with it the assumption that individuals can be repeatedly wounded by unjust social structures and suffer continued psychic distress as a result. In "Not Outside the Range: One Feminist's Perspective on Psychic Trauma," Laura Brown observes that traditional definitions of trauma in psychiatric manuals have defined the term from a white, bourgeois, male perspective as arising from experiences outside the range of "what is normal and usual in the lives of men of the dominant class: white, young, able-bodied, educated, middle-class, Christian men" (101). Thus, because war, genocide, accidents, and natural disasters disrupt bourgeois, male lives, these become legitimate sites of trauma. But when the traumatic symptoms of nightmare, flashback, hypervigilance, and disturbed sleep appear in raped and battered women or exploited workers struggling in grinding poverty, victims are often blamed for bringing on the circumstances of their distress. For Brown, expanding the definition of trauma to include the daily violences inflicted on women and girls, people of color, queer people, the impoverished, and the differently abled exposes oppressive social structures so that they can no longer be viewed as benign and normal. In "Trauma Is as Trauma Does," Maurice Stevens observes that "existing discourses intended to take up issues of history, memory, trauma, and 'therapeutic intervention' have remained primarily silent on questions of racialized or intersectional experience or the importance of difference" (21):

> one does not hear many clinicians or academic traumatists discuss the traumatogenic nature of institutionalized modes of psychic denigration that take the form of race-, class-, gender-, and sexuality-based patterns of social differentiation. Instead, one sees the proliferation of discussions about trauma, memory, and historiography that assume a racially unmarked citizen-subject both in the academy and in clinical settings that is understood to respond in various ways to forces overwhelming. (21)

For Stevens, the work of transforming "the denigrated and degraded" into "whole beings who possess the stuff of historical merit" (21) has been taken up most effectively by writers, artists, and performers whose cultural productions represent and work through the aftershocks of structural violences experienced by marginalized populations.

Meehan's recovery of images of class violence not only exposes brutal power relations but also expands what counts as a "grievable life" (Butler 20). By writing working-class lives onto the page, Meehan writes them into existence, making them count. As Judith Butler asks in her study of mourning and grief, *Precarious*

Life: "How do our cultural frames for thinking the human set limits on the kinds of losses we can avow as loss? After all, if someone is lost, and that person is not someone, then what and where is loss, and how does mourning take place?" (32). Here Butler acknowledges the violences that become possible when the lives of individuals in marginalized groups and Othered nations are neither valued nor protected. Such human beings are already violated, and their violation is not grieved because they have never come fully into existence; in Butler's terms, they are not anyone. As novelist Dorothy Allison puts it: "If I live in a world in which my experience is not reflected back to me, then maybe I'm not real enough; maybe I'm not real at all. . . . That is a trauma: to see yourself never in the world" (246). If recovery from trauma involves reclaiming violent experiences so that they can be mourned, Meehan establishes the grounds for grief by representing the working-class life as valuable,.the working-class person as precisely *someone*.

In *Unclaimed Experience: Trauma, Narrative, and History*, Cathy Caruth observes that at the core of the traumatic narratives she studies is "a kind of double telling, the oscillation between a *crisis of death* and the correlative *crisis of life*: between the story of the unbearable nature of an event and the story of the unbearable nature of its survival. These two stories [are] both incompatible and absolutely inextricable" (7). Caruth's psychoanalytic frame leaves her analysis locked in the dualism of "incompatible and absolutely inextricable." Yet in Meehan's *Dharmakaya,* a Buddhist perspective transforms the incompatible into paradox, radically incorporating an awareness of death by inviting it into the midst of life. Moving beyond the dualism of mind/body and life/death, Meehan's work suggests an ideological shift that allows the violent wound to be witnessed through the lens of a spiritual practice that grants the witness herself interpretive power. Since interpretive power or the lack of it is one of the features of class relations, Meehan's Buddhist-inflected socialism provides a radically different approach to trauma than the political neutrality of psychoanalysis.

"BETWEEN BREATH AND NO BREATH"

Buddhism is a useful spiritual practice for resisting a dominant discourse or ideology because its doctrine of maya posits a transitory, insubstantial, and impermanent phenomenal world. A Westerner adopting this philosophy finds additional resources for reading social structures like class systems as arbitrary rather than natural and inevitable. And belief in the insubstantiality of the phenomenal world is linked to the fragility and impermanence of human life. Indeed, the Tibetan Buddhism Meehan evokes in this book is a spirituality with awareness of death always before it. Robert Thurman describes this stance in his translation of *The Tibetan Book of the Dead*:

> Tibetans observe that anyone can die at any time in any place. Our sense of the concreteness of the life situation, of the solidity of the waking world of the five senses and their objects, is a complete error. Nothing that we think we are, do, feel, or have has any essence, substance, stability or solidity. All the somethings in and around us with which we preoccupy ourselves from morning to night are potentially nothing to us. If we died, they would dissolve in our tightest grasp, forgotten if they were in our mind, lost if they were in our hand, faded into blank numbness if they were in our mind and body. Surprisingly, once we become accustomed to the omnipresent possibility of death in life, we feel greatly liberated. We realize we are essentially free at all times in all situations. We realize that all compulsion is only based on the illusion of substantial continuation, enduring substance, binding essence. We become completely immersed in the medium of freedom. (20)

This is a perspective not incompatible with a postmodern sensibility—fluid identities operate within a shifting landscape of arbitrary sign systems. For Meehan's purposes, the potential nothingness of the daily world with which we engage as well as the nothingness of the individual ego, unfixed and without essence, is introduced in her book's epigraphs. "There is nothing you can give a poet; nothing you can take away," she quotes Anna Akhmatova.

And Bob Dylan: "When you got nothing, you got nothing to lose." In Buddhism, of course, and in these epigraphs, nothing is quite a lot to not have. And nothing comes full circle to become everything in mystic union: "a Buddha's perfect wisdom becomes a Truth Body, a Body of Ultimate Reality, in that an enlightened being experiences the whole universe as one with his or her own being" (Thurman 17). This insight is itself dharmakaya (or Truth Body), and we apprehend it most clearly at the moment of death when, as Meehan's final epigraph from Stanislav Grof's commentary on *The Tibetan Book of the Dead* explains, we know ourselves to be beyond birth and death, one with "the Immutable Light," "[t]he Clear Light of the Void." For Buddhists, much depends on this apprehension, for if the epiphany is missed, one's disembodied consciousness must prepare for another round of life's suffering and instruction through reincarnation. Before that crucial moment, in the life one is currently living, enlightenment involves recognizing the changing states of life "as a continual succession of minor births and deaths, so that at any moment we are in an intermediate state between our past actions and our future evolution" (Bowker 974).

By invoking Buddhism as a spiritual practice with political efficacy, Meehan suggests that religion may be appropriated for the work of cultural transformation. As Stuart Hall observed in his discussion of Rastafarians in Jamaica, elements of religious practice may be reorganized to produce new discursive formations: "Anyone interested in the politics of contemporary culture has to recognize the continuing force in modern life of cultural forms which have a prehistory long predating that of our rational systems, and which sometimes constitute the only cultural resources that human beings have to make sense of their world" ("On Postmodernism" 142). Making an alternative sense of the world economically and politically is indeed what many practicing Buddhists do. For example, in his "Economic Aspects of Social and Environmental Violence from a Buddhist Perspective," Sulak Sivaraksa refuses to mince words about the abuses of global capitalism. A violent and unjust system that benefits transnational corporations, "neoliberal capitalism prizes the accumulation of profits over human well-being and environmental sustainability" (47). Avowing that Buddhism recognizes neither classes nor castes and "does not encourage one group to dominate or exploit the other" (50), Sivaraksa argues that the structural violences perpetuated by our global economy, "institutionalized forms of violence involving, for example, women, children, minority groups, low income countries, or the rest of nature," violate Buddhist precepts "to abstain from the taking of life and from taking what has not been given" (51). He suggests as counterpoint to isolated capitalist consumer culture the Buddhist sangha, a small, autonomous, decentralized spiritual community supporting its members in developing critical self-awareness and a lifestyle "simple, content, self-reliant, compassionate, generous, and mindful" (55). Similarly, well aware that global culture threatens "whole-earth exploitation" by transnational capitalism, Paula Meehan believes that global culture also provides the opportunity for an alternative vision: "We've been given a powerful image of connectedness. I think that the move toward a global culture at its best could be a move away from a material culture to a more spiritual culture" (O'Halloran and Maloy 5).

DHARMAKAYA

Paula Meehan opens *Dharmakaya* with a poem of the same title advising the reader how to meet the moment of death as well as how to meet all those moments in life *before* death; indeed, the poem manages to sustain both perspectives so that the small deaths in an already transitory, insubstantial, and impermanent life become only another version of the big death at the end of human life:

> **Dharmakaya**
> *for Thom McGinty*
>
> When you step out into death
> with a deep breath,

the last you'll ever take
in this shape,

remember the first step on the street—
the footfall and the shadow
of its fall—into silence. Breathe
slow-

ly out before the foot finds solid earth again,
before the city rain
has washed all trace
of your step away.

Remember a time in the woods, a path
you walked so gently
no twig snapped
no bird startled.

Between breath and no breath
your hands cupped your own death,
a gift, a bowl of grace
you brought home to us—

become a still pool
in the anarchic flow, the street's
unceasing carnival
of haunted and redeemed. (*D* 11)

Dedicated to the Dublin street artist Thom McGinty, who died of AIDS in 1995, this memorial poem fuses the movement of McGinty's slow walking mime with "the Buddhist practice of walking meditation, in which the practitioner synchronizes his breathing with his steps, bringing mindful awareness to every motion" (Howard 4). Celebrating his life by evoking McGinty as an exemplar for meeting death, the poem reflects a Buddhist's perception of the moments of life as intermediate states—between past and present, between life and death, between breaths, between one literal step and another, between sound and silence, word and suffix, stillness and flow, order and carnival, haunted and redeemed. In the intermediate state of the present moment, "between breath and no breath," McGinty is represented as bringing home the gift of dharmakaya, an awareness of his own death, from moment to moment and finally. The awareness is called a "gift" and "a bowl of grace"; it provides a saving detachment, registered by the pool that remains still in the face of what is "anarchic" and "unceasing." And this seems a state of mind and being that can go anywhere, that does not require the more familiar Western images of respite in secluded sacred or domestic spaces. Rather, the "you" of the poem has his being in the street, the city, the woods. Other images in the poem register the transitory, the insubstantial, and the impermanent—the moment ending, the life ending, the footstep erased by rain, the path traveled without evidence one has been there. Remember, breathe, remember, become: the narrator intones imperatives and the four-line stanzas arrange themselves as regularly as breaths. Even the pattern of slant rhymes reinforces the sense of an ordering perspective in the midst of the chaotic. Though the poem's variable line lengths suggest free verse, the stanzas unfold first in couplets and then in rhyming alternating lines. The poem's only exact rhyme—death/breath—emphasizes again the close proximity of life and death and of death in life.

What is anarchic, carnivalesque, haunted, and sometimes redeemed appears in the next nine poems of the volume as domestic violence and class trauma. Indeed, the arrangement of poems in Meehan's book suggests that dharmakaya enables the narrator to enter and re-enter the world of suffering with a detachment sufficient to supply a steady hand and a clear eye. In "The View from Under the Table," a child emerges from her hiding place under the kitchen table to find solace in her grandmother's lap: "Somewhere, elsewhere, my mother was sulking in the rain. I call up / her young face. Who did she think she was with her big words / and

her belt and her beatings?" (*D* 12). The child is too frightened by
her mother's violence to confess the real source of her fear to her
grandmother, and she invents shadows and ghosts to explain her
hiding. But the poem witnesses to the ways the child's abuse is
re-experienced as trauma by the narrator in the present. And the
terror and conflict involved in naming the violence is powerfully
evoked in the closing lines: "Who do I think I am to write her? /
She must have been sad. She must have been lonely. / Discipline.
Chastisement. I stretch out my four year old hands" (*D* 12).
Here the narrator still questions her own authority to name the
violence inflicted on her as a child. The hands stretched out for
punishment are those of the traumatized child still present in the
narrator who nonetheless finds the courage to feel compassion for
her mother and speculate about what motivated her violence: sad-
ness, loneliness, and, as we know from other poems, poverty. In
this way the poem witnesses and grieves the abuse of a child and
thereby breaks the silence the child of the poem feels she must
keep. Thus, the poem performs a social act by acknowledging
and expressing what Cassie Premo Steele has called "legacies of a
history of violence." Identifying a continuum where all violences
meet, whether domestic violence, race violence, class violence, or
homophobic violence, Steele argues that "[h]istory is a problem
when it is not remembered and worked through but is repeated
and used to inflict further violence. History may be a solution if
we remember, witness, and mourn our traumatic past" (12). In
Buddhist terms, the act of witness the poem performs might be
read as a gesture toward "perfect compassion," "a limitless embodiment that reaches out from the enlightened being's blissful
oneness with the ultimate reality of freedom to help countless
other beings escape from suffering by realizing their own oneness
with freedom" (Thurman 17).

In "Fist," the adult narrator finds personal memories of her own
childhood wounds evoked by moments of public violence in the
present. Violences meet: the memory of the child's "bloody mouth
a rose suddenly blooming" appears when "you present your hand

to me / as fist, as threat, as weapon" (*D* 13). But here the narrator is explicit about the power of poetry to reclaim a history of violence and thereby heal rather than repeat the past: "this poem, like most that I write, / is a way of going back into the past / I cannot live with and by transforming that past / change the future of it" (*D* 15). The role of Buddhist practice is also made explicit in this process of reclamation in a poem like "Take a breath. Hold it. Let it go," where the narrator grieves over her younger sister, elsewhere described as rising early to catch the factory bus and as "my frail, my breaking sister" (*D* 17). The description of conscious breathing as it is practiced in meditation becomes the metaphor for an older sister who must let go of the belief that she can protect her sibling from a literal fall from "the narrow breeze block fence" or the larger falls the poem implies come later: "I've tried to bawl out, dance out, weep. / The inarticulate foolish gestures of grief. / She falls anyway. I could not save her. / Then or now" (*D* 15). The necessary distance these narrators achieve from mothers and sisters is hard won.

In "Thunder in the House" the permeable boundaries between public and private appear again as the child in the poem overhears the repeated beatings of another child in the flat above, a twelve-year-old child like herself. The narrator's parents refuse to intervene: "My mother had no answers, or if she knew, / was leaving well enough alone. My own father / got cranky and threatened to settle his hash. God / love her, they'd say, she has nobody else. It'd go / even harder on her if anyone interfered" (*D* 21). The narrator continues to live with the shaking ceiling, the humming windows, the audible curses and smacks as well as an internalized sense of helplessness in the face of violence—there are no resources, no aid. Even the remedy of a friendship is lost when the beaten girl serves up what she's been given, robbing the narrator of "my message money. A slide from my plait. / My blue scarf " (*D* 20).

These poems stand alongside depictions of other humiliations in lives defined by poverty and need as in "My Father's Hands That Winter," where the narrator's unemployed father takes up work as a turkey plucker at Christmas: "His hands were swollen, scratched raw and bloody / from the sharp ends of feather, of sinew, / of tendon, from the fourteen-hour day, / from the bite of the boss" (*D* 23). Yet here the class exploitation the father suffers in his public life is not revisited on children in the home. In contrast to his own wounded hands, he protects theirs, boiling up eggs for their coat pockets and supplying old socks "to guard against chilblains." The father's sacrifice is answered in the following stanzas by the narrator's ability and determination to explore the past "at leisure and at will / by pushing on the unlatched tenement door."

ARS POETICA

In the face of powerlessness enforced by class prejudice, poetry becomes the narrator's way of "transforming that past" by speaking back. In "The Exact Moment I Became a Poet" (a poem that echoes Eavan Boland's seizure of the terms of national self-definition in "In Which the Ancient History I Learn Is Not My Own"), Meehan takes up the struggle for self-definition *within* Ireland, on behalf of "mothers, aunts and neighbours / trussed like chickens / on a conveyor belt":

The Exact Moment I Became a Poet
for Kay Foran

was in 1963 when Miss Shannon
rapping the duster on the easel's peg
half obscured by a cloud of chalk

said *Attend to your books, girls,*
or mark my words, you'll end up
in the sewing factory.

It wasn't just that some of the girls'
mothers worked in the sewing factory
or even that my own aunt did,

and many neighbours, but
that those words 'end up' robbed
the labour of its dignity.

Not that I knew it then,
not in those words—labour, dignity.
That's all back construction,

making sense; allowing also
the teacher was right
and no one knows it like I do myself.

But: I *saw* them: mothers, aunts and neighbours
trussed like chickens
on a conveyor belt,

getting sewn up the way my granny
sewed the sage and onion stuffing
in the birds.

Words could pluck you,
leave you naked,
your lovely shiny feathers all gone. (*D* 24)

In this poem the beginnings of class consciousness coincide with the call of vocation; the narrator's identity as poet cannot be separated from her sense of herself as working class. The etymological connection between social position and educational grouping is played out here as the classroom becomes the site of transmission of middle-class values, values the narrator resists because they ask her to degrade and deny her own experience and that of the relatives and neighbors in her community. Raymond Williams describes an essential ambiguity carried by the history of the word *class* through its association with both rank and economic relationships: "The middle class, with which the earners of salaries normally aligned themselves, is an expression of relative social position and thus of social distinction. The working class, specialized from the different notion of the useful or productive classes, is an expression of economic relationships" (65). When Meehan's narrator describes labor robbed of its dignity, she objects to the notion that certain types of labor are assigned a social position and devalued if that social position is low. If factory work confers on one a certain social rank, indeed, work becomes a marker of a social rank; however well one performs that work or however essential that work might be to others is lost. Understanding both the teacher's accuracy in describing class conditions as well as her class prejudice, the narrator chooses the middle way of language, constructing poems that at once witness to class oppression and write narrators and readers beyond it. If, as Meehan says, "Words could pluck you, / leave you naked, / your lovely shiny feathers all gone," the words in her own poems restore dignity and complexity to lives overlooked.

Again and again in this volume Meehan's narrators employ language as oppositional discourse that witnesses to class oppression by recording the damage done. In "Literacy Class, South Inner City," grown women recount the abuses suffered as children in Catholic school, "welts festering" on palms for misspellings, soiled underwear worn on the head. Ignoring the cold of their underheated adult education classrooms, these women sit in their coats and scarves, bending "to the work / of mending what is broken in us. . . . [W]ith no time to waste now, we plant / words on these blank fields" (D 51). In "Swallows and Willows," a teacher's attempt to contain and punish a young woman's sexual energy—caught "at the corner / with the curly headed green eyed boy" (D 53)—is thwarted when the narrator deploys language on her own behalf. Confined in detention and assigned "a verse of a poem," written "[a] hundred times," the narrator usurps the teacher's authority by ignoring a selection "from a *set* text," retrieving instead from her own memory lines from Sylvia Plath's "The Jailer" that "wish him dead or away." These poems represent the classroom as a contested space that at once schools its subjects into class hierarchy even as it offers the wily tools for resistance.

NEITHER CLASS MOBILITY NOR ROMANTIC LOVE

Although the tone and subjects of *Dharmakaya* are courageously demanding for both poet and reader, we shouldn't feel that Meehan's Buddha never laughs. Indeed, her narrators are no more interested in the uncritical adoption of a spiritual code than they are in an unconscious class politics. In this sense, we might say that no subject in this volume is entirely sacred. Her wonderfully ribald "The Tantric Master" is a mock Kama Sutra, playfully cataloguing a lover's body and the pleasures it brings:

> His mouth, I won't go into, being all cliché in the face of it,
> except to say the dip of his lip is most suited to suction and
>   friction,
> and other words ending in tion, tion, tion, which come to
>   think of it
> when I'm in the grip of it, is exactly how I make sweet moan.
>   For I shall consider
> him whizzbang dynamo and hellbent on improving my
>   spiritual status. (*D* 39)

Here Meehan's narrator isn't interested in an enlightenment that transcends the body; unlike the tantric masters who use ritualized sex to move beyond the corporeal, her narrator declares, "The best that I hope for in our daily instructions / is the lull between breaths, spent and near pacified" (*D* 40). With the image of the in-between in "lull between breaths," Meehan again invokes dharmakaya. But it is the realm of sexual love and its aftermath that presents the greatest challenges in this volume's later poems to the Buddhist spiritual practice of nonattachment.

In "Sudden Rain" the narrator flatly declares, "I'm no Buddhist: too attached to the world / of my six senses." Here the senses ostensibly luxuriate in an "unexpected shower," but it's not sensual pleasure in the natural world that a Buddhist practice would ask the narrator to forsake. Rather, the real source of suffering is revealed in the closing lines as the desperate desire for the beloved to "be tender and never fickle" (*D* 49). Elsewhere in this sonnet sequence, instructively titled "Suburb," the narrator describes herself "coiled / in a foetal crouch behind the couch" after a devastating fight with a lover. The poems in this series explode the notion that one might find safe haven within the confines of either the middle-class suburb or the romantic relationship. In "Stink Bomb" a retreat into private life is represented as dangerous isolation where the narrator is left vulnerable to her lover's rage, cut off from communal resources that themselves turn malevolent when Halloween trick-or-treaters are ignored. Indeed, these sonnets are ironic love poems to an arid landscape populated by teenage vandals and malicious gossips. In this land of isolated individualism, Meehan's narrator is left confused about where her loyalties might lie; in "Pyrolarty" she protects, by her silence, the vandals who have stolen a neighbor's wheelie bin and burned it, even though she has to "claw / the washing in" (*D* 46) amid the toxic fumes of burning plastic. The bourgeois remedy of seeking security in property and possessions fails either to inspire community or to protect: kids gather "pallets and cast-off furniture, the innards of sheds," steal and ignite wheelie bins, and throw stink bombs when denied Halloween candy. As if to demonstrate how inhospitable the narrator finds this suburban terrain to spiritual growth, the Buddhist refrain reappears drained of meaning and depth. In "Mistle Thrush," the narrator monotones, "Dying is simple. You breathe in, you breathe out, you breathe in, / you breathe out and you don't breathe in again" (*D* 48). When not accosted by wayward adolescents, these narrators threaten to die of boredom. Class trauma has revealed another face: isolation, stagnation, spiritual death.

Suggesting that neither class mobility nor bourgeois values can effectively provide a location from which to speak, the penultimate poem in *Dharmakaya*, "It Is All I Ever Wanted," presents a narrator ventriloquizing another voice before reclaiming her own. Dedicated to Meehan's Irish literary foremother, Eavan Boland, the poem opens with a signature Boland scene, the poet at her desk musing over "my native city, its hinterland / and backstreets and river scored." But the poem takes a dramatic turn, moving from the domestic to the feral, at once paying homage to Boland and also announcing the narrator's decision to claim the difference of her own subjects:

> Last week I took as metaphor, or at least as sign,
> a strange meeting:
> a young fox walking the centre line
>
> down the south side of the Square
> at three in the morning.
> She looked me clear
>
> in the eyes, both of us curious
> and unafraid. She was saying—
> or I needed her to say—*out of the spurious*
>
> *the real, be sure*
> *to know the value of the song*
> *as well as the song's true nature.*
>
> Be sure, my granny used to say,
> of what you're wanting,
> for fear you'd get it entirely.
>
> Be sure, I tell myself,
> you are suffering
> animal like the fox, not nymph
>
> nor sylph, nor figment,
> but human heart breaking
> in the silence of the street.
>
> Familiar who grants me the freedom of the city,
> my own hands spanning
> the limits of pity. (*D* 62)

Here the fox as familiar evokes the shape-shifters of Irish legend—the narrator is both likened to and spoken to by the fox. The transformative power of the shape-shifter becomes an emblem for what Meehan has tried to do in her poems—transform trauma by witnessing to class violence. As Meehan puts it: "You can take even the very elements that oppress you and turn them into something powerful and good" (O'Halloran and Maloy 13). In this poem, too, we return to Granny's voice, folk wisdom, and dialect issuing a homespun warning about the nature and consequences of desire. And this is not desire lived only in private spaces, nor human appointments kept during reasonable hours: the meeting is "strange"; the fox is a "sign"; it is "three in the morning." In the end the poem urges the speaker to resist construction as a bourgeois poet, to speak out of her lived experience as "suffering animal," a position that grants her the freedom to witness. On the city street, in the intermediate space between the left lane and the right, the fox returns us to the volume's opening poem, its public space and spiritual practice.

Just as classism and speciesism inform each other in "The Exact Moment I Became a Poet," this poem, too, connects through proximity the human and the animal. Meehan's narrator meets the fox as respected other in an exchange between equals, each looking the other in the eyes, each "curious and unafraid." The speaker does not assume she knows who the fox is any more than the fox knows the speaker's human identity. And Meehan uses the powerful tool of human language to register its capacity to capture and name for human uses; her speaker identifies the making of a metaphor, the taking of a sign, and catches herself as she gives the fox a message she realizes may be the result of her own human need, acknowledging, "I needed her to say." The midnight meeting with an urban fox who is very much her own animal becomes the occasion for the narrator's exploration of self and other, projection and reflection. Just as she has adjusted her own relation to the fox as other and identified her human capacity to use the fox as a metaphor and a sign, so she realizes that she might resist the same process in naming herself according to received social categories. What the fox brings her is not, then, a symbol but a lived commonality between sentient beings, an identity as "suffering animal" who might make a genuine connection with another living being. The exchange is liberating: "Familiar who grants me the freedom of the city, / my own hands spanning / the limits of pity." With "familiar" Meehan draws on the premodern figure of the wise woman accompanied by animals with whom she shares access to an inner, intuitive wildness, her own animal self. *The Tibetan Book of the Dead* is the popular title of the Buddhist text in the West; in Tibet the volume is known as *The Great Book of Natural Liberation through Understanding of the Between*. Like the fox in the middle of the road in the middle of the night, Meehan's poems work their differences in liminal spaces, where a transforming vision might most powerfully emerge.

INTERVIEW

....

INSIDE THE MASK IS A HUMAN FACE, 2019

PAULA MEEHAN: To be an archivist of community experience? I wouldn't always be satisfied with wanting to write these poems about certain kinds of collisions of class and education. Sometimes I think I'd be better just jettisoning the need to examine the past. Maybe that's what's happening now.

KATHRYN KIRKPATRICK: I keep feeling that I want to know what the new adaptations might be. That interests me the most.

PM: I wonder, is it another form of, say, what the Haida do with their masks? You know, their dance masks. The animal masks that open out and inside the mask is a human face.

KK: Hmmmm.

PM: I mean, do you think you might be doing something like that in poetry, and your animal research, and *Our Held Animal Breath*? It seems like a very ritualized thing. And the closest I've felt, and this is just a feeling rather than a worked-out understanding, but the closest I've felt to that kind of material is in the Haida dances and the stories that go with them, and in the Micmac stories collected by Ruth Whitehead, an anthropologist. It is shape-shifting and the sense that when you leave your house in the morning as a human person, before you come back in you might have been a bear for a while, do you know?

KK: Well, I think because of the legacies of modernity I just feel very focused on trying to let the actual animals show up. It's a mask, but it's not just for me. What would it be like to learn from the kind of shape-shifting that you do in your own poems? I think I started in on my animal poems precisely because of having been through the illness. Talk about embodied. I felt very aware of my animal body and actually grateful for it because, when you're in that kind of struggle, your body just takes over. It has a certain kind of wisdom, and it knows about the wounds that have been inflicted, and I think that it wants to heal them.

PM: I don't use the mask in the way of Yeats, you know, a poet who puts on a mask to speak truth. I mean the animal becomes part of the ritualization; do you know what I mean? You put on the animal, and it is about becoming it.

KK: Right.

PM: I mean the way the mask functions in the dances is a way of storytelling—the way the stories for the Micmac operate in their six worlds of consciousness. They're very sophisticated.

KK: Yes.

PM: But I love that when you open the animal there's just a small human face that is part of the animal. It's like that's part of the animal's imagination, it figures into the animal's imagination. And your work has always been something to pull me, and to push me as well, to examine my own mannerisms, you know. The mannerism seems to be the complete enemy of progress, or of going anywhere interesting anyway. With each spate of making I'm trying to pull back before the poetry becomes mannered or ornamented for its own sake.

KK: I'm always so taken by those birds at the end of "The Exact Moment I Became a Poet." Because I guess what I've written about lately is the proximity of the working women to those dead birds, you know. "The words could pluck you, / leave you naked, / your lovely shiny feathers all gone." The women have become the plucked birds.

PM: Oh, totally. And there's something of that grinding mill—Blake's dark, satanic mills in the old sweatshops. Safety would not have been a big concern. I mean, they were sweatshops and fourteen-year-old girls were children.

KK: So do you not like this phrase "ars poetica"?

PM: I think it's fine.

KK: Okay, but you don't tend to think about your poems that way?

PM: I kind of believe that you're born a poet. It's a mad thing to say, maybe, and maybe everyone was born potentially with an intense relationship with language, I don't know. But you have to be made as well. Maybe for some intense souls it's enough to be born. But I mean the ars poetica in the sense of some attempt to lay the energy down openly and say, "Well this drives me"—whoever me is? Because I think that girl in the poem is also fabricated to serve my purposes like a kind of an avatar, isn't she? A constructed self? I sometimes think of the self as Frankenstein's creature (who always spoke to me of the wounded human or creature), and it's because there's a kind of consciousness that can displace you within your own place. I wonder . . . that's a question I ask myself: "Would I have been better not being driven, I don't know, to certain kinds of poetry?" I don't know. Who knows, at the moment I might have a period of doubt, so I'm going to be doubting everything.

KK: But don't you think that that's our times?

PM: Mmm. I mean, I'm seeing doubt as positive—part of the work being to question every single thing. Well, I mightn't be getting a lot of comfort from the way I'm thinking about things at a particular moment, and then I realize I don't actually *want* comfort, you know? I want to stay fit for the journey, as I said before. Be there, ready and able, for whatever shows up.

KK: Yes, the readiness.

PM: Is every poem also an ars poetica, do you think?

KK: I know, and what is it about setting out a program? I mean, I named one of my poems "Ars Poetica," and it was about feeling that I needed to trace back all the clothes on my back to where they came from. Where did the cotton come from, and who made the piece of clothing? Imagining the materials and the labor—that complicated enormously, you know, any kind of joy I was feeling. I feel like, for me, I've always been writing at the margins of an empire. I guess that's a good place to stand if you're also trying to witness.

2

RESISTING ENVIRONMENTAL INJUSTICE

———

In her 1999 stage play *Cell,* Paula Meehan presents four Irish women whose only access to the nonhuman world of nature is through a prison window. Within the microcosm of the cell, a class system has developed where heroin dealer Delo dominates and exploits her young cellmates by using their drug addictions to force them to perform sexual favors and smuggle messages. Making use of the nonhuman in much the same way she makes use of humans, Delo disassociates herself from her most brutal acts of violence toward her cellmates by calling on Snakey, a large snake tattooed on her arm, to terrorize them; her cellmates, on the other hand, display a marked sensitivity to the natural world. For example, Lila, a nineteen-year-old Dublin woman sentenced to three years for possession of heroin, maintains an intimate relationship with a natural world, despite her agoraphobia, that she experiences as animate:

It's the humour of the day as much as anything else. Today is [. . .] sulky. There are big black clouds away over there where the canal should be. Jesus Martha, it's beautiful—there's a full moon up. In the daytime, imagine. Isn't that a brilliant thing. It's like you can look right through it [. . .] And there's the edge of that big tree. The weeping willow in the back garden at the other end. Very sad looking. The leaves beginning to fall. Yellow they are now. Annie loved that tree. And I can see the top-half of a lamppost with the election poster with your woman's face on it [. . .] wait a minute [. . .] A New Ireland. Forward to [. . .] something. I can't make it out. I wish I could see more of the garden. (*Cell* 20)

Despite her passionate engagement with the landscape outside her cell window, Lila's view is limited by her subject location as an imprisoned working-class woman. The New Ireland of the 1990s Celtic Tiger boom is as hidden from her as Eden itself. So deeply has Lila internalized the systems of oppression by which she is victimized that she cannot even envision this new economic Eden, much less participate in it. Delo, in her mimicking of bourgeois property relations, has limited her cellmates' access to the outdoors by owning the window and the bunk below, even though she does not value the view. Her portrayal suggests that the true criminal mirrors the dominant order, a point the play's hero, Alice, reiterates when she identifies the "real crooks" as including "the politicians themselves" (*Cell* 37). By identifying the doomed Lila so closely with a marginalized natural world, Meehan suggests that the price of a New Ireland in an era of global capitalism is the perpetuation of both social injustice and environmental degradation.

In the context of the 2008 financial crash and beyond, Meehan's play was prescient. Members of the Irish government agency Combat Poverty had published a special report in 2001 describing Ireland as having "one of the highest levels of income inequality in the European Union": "the gap between rich and poor actually grew in the 1990s." Indeed, as Kieran Keohane and Carmen Kuhling observe, amid economic crisis and the subsequent austerity measures, the global plutonomy flourished, the Forbes Rich List of 2011 identifying "a 10 percent rise in the number of billionaires since 2008, with their net worth rising quickly and steadily" (3). In Ireland, where in 2010 "the richest one per cent of the population owned 34 per cent of the national wealth" (11), the government pursued an IMF-ECB-EU (International Monetary Fund-European Central Bank-European Union) bailout by cutting social services rather than increasing taxes on the rich. Alison Spillane argues that the "slashing of funding to state-supported equality, poverty and women's organizations" during the financial crisis amounted to "structural violence against women in Ireland" (159) where austerity measures "had a noticeably gendered effect, with poorer women bearing the brunt of the burden" (151). Michael Cronin, in "Ireland's Disappeared: Suicide, Violence and Austerity," writes that countries facing the most serious financial reversals like Greece and Ireland also suffered the greatest rises in suicide rates (134) with the poor ten times more at risk than the more affluent (135). Meanwhile, Ireland's super-rich "cosmopolitan tax exiles" (6) live as the country's latest absentee landlords in London, Manhattan, and the Cayman Islands. This is the economic context in which "post-Celtic Tiger Ireland [became] a haunted landscape of ghost estates and Zombie banks cannibalizing the state" (9).

The economic boom that exacerbated class inequities also triggered ecological crisis. As geographer Mark Boyle charted the conditions before the 2008 crash in "Cleaning Up after the Celtic Tiger," economically pressured Tiger states threaten the human populations they ostensibly serve, through

> historically unprecedented transformations of nature, transformations that have been coloured by the tendency of the Tigers to house a disproportionate number of global investments in the "dirty industries" [. . .] The result [. . .] has been that export oriented industrialization has telescoped into three decades processes of environmental destruction that took many more years to unfold in earlier industrializing societies. (175)

For Boyle, natural processes help constitute social and political processes, and ignoring nature as an actor in human affairs can well guarantee disasters. He defines the natural processes in which humans intervene as "socio-nature," open to influence but not necessarily to control: "Socio-nature has agency precisely because it impinges upon, disturbs, outwits, and occasionally poisons the very accumulation strategy that gave birth to it" (176). Thus, in their vastly and, one might add, rashly accelerated rates of development, Tiger states have given us a magnified view of the perils of industrial capitalism. By ignoring nature's agency as "alive, sensitive, and responsive to human actions" (173) and subscribing to what environmental historian Carolyn Merchant has described as "a mechanistic universe.... filled with dead and passive matter," we create the terms for commercial capitalism's "exploitation of nature and human beings as resources" (Merchant, *Death of Nature* 190). Indeed, philosopher Karen Warren uses the phrase "woman—other human Other—nature interconnec- tions" (21) to describe the various ways that not only nature but also "women and tribal and peasant societies embedded in nature" are often read as resources ripe for exploitation (26). This devaluing of women, other human Others, and nature has meant, according to environmental justice critic T. V. Reed,

> that for decades the worst forms of environmental degradation have been enabled by governmental and corporate policies of dumping problems on communities of color, poor whites, and the Third World. This process was inadvertently aided and abet- ted by mainstream environmentalists whose not-in-my-back- yard focus led to more sophisticated corporate and governmental efforts at environmental cover-ups that mollify the middle classes while intensifying distress in poor communities in the United States and around the world. (14)

Growing up in just such a distressed poor community, Meehan has, through her work, long given readers access to imaginative refigur- ings of women—other human Other—nature interconnections. I call hers an ecofeminist poetics.

ECOFEMINIST POETICS
In their interview with Meehan published in *Contemporary Liter- ature*, Eileen O'Halloran and Kelli Maloy described the poet as

"called to record a Dublin that is disappearing as a result of the 'Celtic Tiger,' Ireland's . . . multinational economic boom" (2). Meehan has seen the leveling of her working-class neighborhood near the docks as part of a new colonization of the area by multinational corporations: "after you're decolonized from one power, you're recolonized by another. It sometimes feels that in our case we're just now part of the economy of the evil empire; transnational capitalism rules all" (O'Halloran and Maloy 5). In the face of her Dublin community's unemployment, despair, and a heroin addiction epidemic brought on by the displacement and decline of traditional industries, Meehan records in her poems the richness of a vanished childhood community, a community she credits with providing elements of a precolonial imaginative world:

> The women in my family were incredibly witchy, everything was a sign of something else. For instance, if a bird flew against a window, it was a sign of death visiting the house. Nothing was just as it seemed, everything had to be interpreted, which is fairly like what I do now. One of the central facts in poetry is that it talks about one thing in terms of another. So the women around were all the time dealing in signs, and certainly that must have been a very strong influence. (O'Halloran and Maloy 5)

This willingness to weave precolonial and premodern ways of knowing with a modern secular rationalism and a socialist politics lends Meehan's poems to ecofeminist readings. Indeed, socialist ecofeminists Maria Mies and Vandana Shiva suggest that the combining of "contemporary science, technologies, and knowledge with ancient wisdom, traditions and even magic" (8) helps move us beyond dualisms of culture/nature, mind/body, and reason/ feeling that foster the oppression of women, other human Others, and nature. Such binaries are central to the cosmology of a capitalist patriarchal world system that defines freedom as the transcendence of nature, a transcendence available only for a few and at the expense of the Others. Alternatively, Mies and Shiva's "subsistence perspective" urges a redefinition of "freedom" such that what Marx terms the realm of necessity—where we labor to secure the food, water, and shelter necessary for survival—grounds every human life, thus helping to create just and sustainable social and ecological worlds. "Freedom *within* the realm of necessity can be universalized to all; freedom *from* necessity can be available to only a few" (8).

This reframing of the exploitation of nature as inseparable from class exploitation is central to Meehan's vision as well. Indeed, her work offers a broad challenge to a range of binaries that maintain class, gender, and species privilege. Although her writing is profoundly associated with the city of Dublin, her poems unsettle any stark opposition between country and city, not least by a frequent confounding of public and private space, of indoors and outdoors. Moreover, throughout her work, Meehan represents animals, wild and undomesticated, as fellow travelers in an often harsh patriarchal capitalist culture. In this chapter I explore the ways an "urban" poet writing from the location of working-class women represents nature as unappropriable other. Occupying a space outside the bourgeois construction of nature (as separate and subordinate), Meehan's poems represent the human and nonhuman in intimate relation, sustained paradoxically by a tension between the known and unknowable. This acknowledging of and respect for otherness re-enacts a re-enchantment of the natural world and becomes a way of framing a fundamental wildness that is also an irreducible otherness existing in the self. Approached in this way, nature emerges in Meehan's poems as an indominable context for the knowing subject who is both led and transformed by a fitful mixture of agency and mystery; the process is often figured in her work as shape-shifting—the human and nonhuman alternately transmogrified—the trope that fascinated Meehan in Gary Snyder's work with Indigenous American cultures, which inspired her to re-embrace the shape-shifting traditions in Irish legend and myth for her own writing.

OUTSIDE/INSIDE

In Meehan's first collection, *Return and No Blame*, the narrator of "The Apprentice" identifies herself as a city child removed to the suburban housing estate, much as Meehan herself relocated from her inner-city neighborhood to the working-class district of Finglas. "A city slum child thrown / into a roomier ghetto," the narrator embraces the image of the 1916 socialist martyr James Connolly even as she quarrels with the specter of Yeats, who looks out "from high Georgian windows" at a debased city poor, "clowns" in his "private review." Certain she must be wary of the masters who would ask her to be blind to class privilege, the narrator proclaims her difference as a working-class poet in solidarity with women, not "swanlike" but "hollow of cheek with poverty / and the whippings of history!" (*RNB* 27). Like many of Meehan's narrators, this one speaks outside the domestic enclosure of bourgeois privilege, literally walking "new laid roads," haunted by the voices of the city slum and led by the mysterious out-of-doors: "Strange the things that reach my ears—/ A voice that whispered in the ditch / A secret up through chance and time / To make a rhyme, a chant for me" (*RNB* 28). Here the poet steps aside from a received bourgeois literary tradition and apprentices herself to the difference of her own lived experiences as a working-class woman. And those experiences include the murmurings of an animated natural world, "strange" and "secret," whose agency the poet combines with her own "to make a rhyme, a chant."

Meehan has noted that women's historical disenfranchisement has taught them alternative relationships to place, beyond ownership and even attachment:

> Our experience of ownership of land or territory is nonexistent. I do not have a sense of owning. I don't own a house, land, a proper native place. Even though I could say Dublin and the language spoken there is one of our biggest honours, I'm much more interested in inner space: the emotional or psychic wilderness rather than the physical one. (Praga 80)

Located by gender and class outside possessive individualism's investment in private property, Meehan is twice-othered, a condition that leads her to awareness of the wilderness within. In "Southside Party," such a perspective allows an undomesticated narrator to reject romantic interludes with privileged men: "No sir, I'm not your little baby, / Your little honey sweet and sugary, / Not the icing on *your* bun, son. / Not *your* pretty gal, pal" (*RNB* 17).

Throughout this first volume, women have their being most happily in the out-of-doors. In the opening sequence, "Echoes," women gathered in the backyard are the source of tribal news for a young girl who knows that if she gets "real quiet / And unnoticed" she will overhear communal secrets, "strange tales of babies / And blood and screams in the night / And stuff about strikes and lockouts too" (*RNB* 11). Indoors, on the other hand, is the location of family dramas and gender politics, as in the closing poem of this sequence where the narrator recalls her father's response to a missed curfew: "At two o'clock he shook the clock / Into my tiptoeing face / And hurled it through the window / Rather than hurl me" (*RNB* 13). Here the undomesticated woman's failure to obey the father's rule of law results in the threat of permanent displacement from whatever protections that space might offer. As the clock alarm rings in her yard outside the broken window, the daughter loads a gun in her dreams against the paternal threats to her autonomy and aspirations.

Another stultifying domestic interior is evoked in "Journey to My Sister's Kitchen," where a sister tends "to things that hold the necessary for living"—crockery and cutlery, doors and floors "scrubbed, waxed, and polished," the sister herself silent and deadened. The narrator feels so trapped by this interior space that she grows afraid whenever she approaches it and is never entirely sure she will get away: "Oh sister, I am afraid of my face in the mirror / Lest it stay when I have gone" (*RNB* 19). For those who don't get away, as in the poem "Moving," one domestic space is much like another, the change of residence for the victimized woman amounting only to a "brand new nightmare." In this poem the brutalization of women is likened to the brutalization of animals in the abattoir, "where blood and screams / Are made as commonplace / As sticks, as stones, as tea" (*RNB* 23). Both violences are normalized by their frequency, the slaughter of animals and the beating of women making the ordinary brutal and the brutal ordinary.

"INSTRUCTIONS TO AN ABSENT HUSBAND" AS ECOFEMINIST POETICS

In "Instructions to an Absent Husband," a poem in Meehan's second collection, *Reading the Sky*, the narrating wife leaves a recipe for her betraying spouse to roast her like a dead deer:

> You open the hated book:
> It is the book of my self.
> The more that you read there
> The fainter the print becomes
> Until the letters are bleached
> White nests protected by the page.

> I gave up the window box:
> Leaves went transparent,
> Eaten away by greenfly.
> When you come home you'll find
> Geranium ghosts, spectral nasturtiums,
> A flock of albino butterflies
> Settled on the sill. I'll be hung

> Up in the larder by the heels,
> Dressed as a deer would be,
> My skin in a casual heap on the floor.
> You can wear it if you wish
> Though the skin clings to parts,
> Especially the extremities. Still,
> A sharp flint stone could do the trick.

It should be a comfortable fit.
There's a note in the dresser
On French seams and buttonholes
Lest you need to alter any part.
The breasts will be a problem I foresee.
You'll need the smallest crewel for the job
And the good new scissors of German steel.
The offcuts may be useful somewhere else.

Put the rest of me on at gas mark three
(You know those stringy muscles in my back!)
Don't forget to baste me now and then.
Don't bring your current lover home to tea.
There's just enough for one. Besides
I'm an acquired taste, like squid
Or pickled limes. I wouldn't delay—
Were I you I'd catch the earliest ferry
Else the worms will have their way with me.

You'd come upon me bleached and empty
In the cool larder rafters, the slates blown down,
The green garden light nesting in my bones.
    (*RS* 34–35)

In a dramatic series of shape-shiftings, the narrator initially appears as a book in the process of being unwritten, each page erased by the husband as he reads, "Until the letters are bleached / White nests protected by the page." Reduced to a substantial blankness, the abandoned woman reappears as the memory of an untended window box, geraniums and nasturtiums devoured by greenfly. Then the devouring greenfly become the monstrosity of the devouring husband confronted with his wife "hung // Up in the larder by the heels, / Dressed as a deer would be." Self and other continue to shift as the husband is invited to wear the wife's discarded skin, and the congruity of wife as deer becomes the incongruity of husband as wife. The wife's skin is only a comfortable fit if it is altered in a mutilation and erasure of the female body by "[a] sharp flint stone" and "the good new scissors of German steel." Roasted, the female body is transformed again, this time by an oven at gas mark three, and she is likened briefly to "squid / Or pickled lime" before her final manifestation as food for worms and, finally, bleached bones in the "cool larder rafters, the slates blown down, / The green garden light nesting in my bones." Here the wife's ability to assume many shapes is in marked contrast to the husband's fixed identity. No selkie, he will not be transformed by a new skin; rather, he will alter it elaborately so that it fits the man he already is. Unable and unwilling to shape-shift, he lacks the radical empathy that might have sustained a marriage. On one level, the myriad images of transformation link the wife's body with the natural world of process and decay. As if to salvage something from the husband's abuse and neglect, the narrator converts the bitter ingredients of her marriage into the macabre practicality of a meal, making herself willing prey. But while the wife in this poem has agency, orchestrating and documenting her own death and renaming her body as food, the poem's ability to unsettle and disturb comes precisely from its striking transposition of female and animal bodies.

As Carol J. Adams and Josephine Donovan observe in their introduction to *Animals and Women*, women's bodies have long been equated with animality, an equation made possible by gendering reason and rationality as male in an "ideology of transcendent dualism" (2). This dualism appears in the familiar binaries of culture/nature and mind/body, where women, along with other human Others, animals, and the natural world, collectively occupy the degraded space against which the subject formation of men as rational originators and arbiters of culture unfolds:

Historically, the ideological justification for women's alleged inferiority has been made by appropriating them to animals: from Aristotle on, women's bodies have been seen to intrude upon

their rationality. Since rationality has been construed by most
Western theorists as the defining requirement for membership in
the moral community, women—along with nonwhite men and
animals—were long excluded. Until the twentieth century this
"animality" precluded women's being granted the rights of public
citizenship. (1)

I would argue that Meehan's "Instructions to the Absent Husband"
radically exposes the ideology of transcendent dualism which Adams
and Donovan find "at the root of both the oppression of women and
the exploitation of nature, including animals" (1). Indeed, Meehan's
poem is challenging because the very emotions it evokes expose our
complicity as readers in the systems of oppression we ostensibly abhor.
The routine use of animals as clothing and food is horrific because
applied to a human being, "skin in a casual heap on the floor," "the
rest of me on at gas mark three / (You know those stringy muscles in
my back!)" Yet the narrator suggests that her own debased Otherness
relies precisely on her bodily connection with the deer, an animal as
easily exploited as she has been and by the same systems of value.

While Adams and Donovan locate the transcendent dualism
that disenfranchises women, other human Others, and nature in
a Western tradition of hierarchical values, feminist anthropologist
Sherry Ortner, in her classic essay "Is Female to Male as Nature Is
to Culture?," observes a similar tendency in non-Western societies
to position women closer to nature because of their physical capacity for childbirth:

Woman's physiology, more involved more of the time with "species life"; woman's association with the structurally subordinate domestic context, charged with the crucial function of
transforming animal-like infants into cultural beings; "woman's
psyche", appropriately molded to mothering functions by her so-
cialization and tending toward greater personalism and less mediated modes of relating—all these factors make woman *appear*

to be rooted more directly and deeply in nature. (Ortner 38; my emphasis)

This *appearance* of a more bodily body, more fully involved with natural processes, allows for the displacement by patriarchal systems of dominance of all that is troubling about living as a mortal creature onto groups of Others. For Ortner, the feminist project involves acknowledging "that the whole scheme is a construct of culture rather than a fact of nature. Woman is not 'in reality' any closer to (or further from) nature than man—both have consciousness, both are mortal" (34). Women along with men occupy mediating roles between culture and nature in what for Ortner is an "ongoing dialectic" between what human labor and intention create of, and in relation to, everything else (35).

By exaggerating her own physicality and frankly naming her female body as animal, Meehan's narrator in "Instructions" literalizes this social construct of woman as closer to nature by extending it to its logical extreme. Located on the other side of the binary, the husband will perform the cultural acts of sewing and cooking with her raw body and skin. The poem thus ventriloquizes a response to the husband's perspective by providing instructions that he has in a sense written himself through his own culturally sanctioned debasement of her. Read in this way, "Instructions to an Absent Husband" serves as a powerful poetic intervention in the politics of transcendent dualism and stands as a prototypical ecofeminist poem. The poem closes with images of liminality, the structures of the house disintegrating so that the borders between self, body, home, and garden dissolve. An animate nature actively nests as "green garden light" in the narrator's bones, making a home with the female body which the husband could not. Ecocritic Neil Evernden has described this blurring of boundaries between self and environment as a feature of animism: "once we engage in the extension of the boundary of the self into the environment, then of course we imbue it with life and can quite properly regard it as animate—it is animate because we are part of it" (101). Reversing the perspective, Edward Abbey has described this boundary blurring beyond the binaries of self and other as "intersubjectivity," the human taking on qualities of the nonhuman, "merging, molecules getting mixed" (qtd. in Scheese 313). By poem's end, a living nature has actively reclaimed the narrator's female body, culminating a grotesque enactment of women's exploitation with an image of that mediated space between human dwelling and wilderness, the garden. Finally, as cultural artifact, "Instructions to an Absent Husband" might be said to function as *sacra*, anthropologist Victor Turner's term for the monstrous and disproportionate images that appear during the transition or liminal state of initiation rites when neophytes are being taught the worldview of their culture (38). Addressed to the absent husband—and by extension to the reader—this disturbing poem functions as a building block of the new cultural myth Meehan wishes to construct, one in which anthropocentric and anthrocentric values are exposed and an animistic vision of human beings in the natural world is restored.

RECLAIMING THE STREET

Feminist geographers have discussed the ways nineteenth-century separate-spheres ideology helped construct bourgeois definitions of private and public space. As Joni Seager and Mona Domosh observe, "The feminine world of home was intended to be the seat of moral, aesthetic, and cultural stability—qualities not furthered in the male world of waged work" (7). Allotted the private sphere of home and family, proper bourgeois women were to be accompanied in public spaces. Even in the twentieth century, when they were increasingly required by a capitalist economy to become consumers, where and when bourgeois women shopped was carefully circumscribed. The unaccompanied streetwalker was, after all, the prostitute, a sexually available and socially polluted Other. For Seager and Domosh, the nineteenth-century strictures banning women from free access to public space continue to be deeply internalized: "Although most violence against women is actually perpetrated in the private spaces of home, it is those spaces defined as 'public' that the majority of women fear most" (100).

Yet in a poem like Meehan's "Buying Winkles," from her collection *The Man Who Was Marked By Winter* (1991), the city street is reclaimed by female agency. Indeed, the streets in this poem are well populated by women that the narrator, who is a child, can "wave up to at sills or those / lingering in doorways." Though she is warned by her mother "don't be talking to strange / men on the way," the poem represents the street as the site of female empowerment and possibility. For the young girl, it's a woman who sends her outdoors for the family meal and a woman who reigns over this public space, "sitting outside the Rosebowl Bar / on an orange-crate, a pram loaded / with pails of winkles before her" (*MMW* 15). Thus, rather than the phallic power often on display in public spaces, this street is populated by winkles (British nursery slang for penis), which turn out to be not only unthreatening but nourishing because the old woman guides the young girl in gaining a kind of hermaphroditic access to them: "Stick it in / till you feel a grip, then slither him out" (*MMW* 15). Successful in her errand, the young girl returns "proudly home," having mastered the threat of a public space, in possession of "newspaper twists / bulging fat with winkles." With the help of other women, especially the crone winkle merchant, she has defused phallic control of the streets and made a place of liberation for herself. Indeed, as feminist geographer Tovi Fenster suggests, women who repeatedly travel urban space make of them personalized places:

> [T]he space shaped by female fear and boldness is the space of female embodied knowledge, an internally contradictory space beyond the mind-body split. It is simultaneously subjective and intersubjective. The women who feel confident reclaim space for themselves through everyday practices and routinized uses. By daring to go out—by their very presence in the urban sphere—women produce space that is more available for other women. Hence, spatial confidence is a "manifestation of power." Walking

on the street can be seen as a political act: women "write themselves onto the street." (263)

By writing her narrators so thoroughly onto the street and into the
out-of-doors, Meehan thus repeatedly challenges any essential identification of women with the domestic enclosure. Indeed, besides the
wide-ranging wise crone, a significant nurturing figure in her later
poems is the father as domestic man.

In the opening poem of *Pillow Talk* (1994), "My Father
Perceived as a Vision of St Francis," the narrator wakes to the
sound of her father in the kitchen: "I heard / him rake the ash
from the grate, / plug in the kettle, hum a snatch of a tune"
(*PT* 11). The father's nurturing gentleness finds dramatic expression in the out-of-doors as he steps into the back garden and is
transformed as Francis of Assisi, "birds / of every size, shape,
colour" appearing to greet him: "The garden was a pandemonium /
when my father threw up his hands / and tossed the crumbs in the
air" (*PT* 12). Later in the volume, in "The Wounded Child," kind
men are evoked as talismans, "a token of a good time, like a //
night under a lucky star, / untroubled, with a gentle man / who
means you no harm" (*PT* 55). Such men, themselves responsive to
an animate, nonhuman world, seem compatible counterparts to
female narrators with a sure sense of their own sexuality. Hence,
the fluid gender boundaries in Meehan's poems create spaces for
both women's agency and reciprocal relations with nature.

We might say, then, that Meehan's poems reappropriate the
figure of the streetwalker by representing women at home in their
own bodies in public spaces. It is true that, in *Pillow Talk*, the
poem "Night Walk" acknowledges the potential danger of the
dark city street where "that poor woman last night" was "dragged
down Glovers Alley, raped there, / battered to a pulp" (*PT* 22), and
in "On Being Taken for a Turkish Woman," the narrator observes,
"there's too much danger at the edges, and I need all my concentration for reading the street" (*PT* 46), but most often Meehan's
narrators attest to the "spatial confidence"(Fenster 263) that comes

from long familiarity with her Dublin streets. As Fenster describes the daily walking practices of the urban woman, "Making the use of space a part of one's daily routine erases the myth of danger from it" (263). So intricate and multilayered does this outdoor knowledge become that in a poem like "A Child's Map of Dublin," an adult narrator preserves her childhood neighborhood by recalling it as she walks through what little remains after gentrification:

> I walk the northside streets that whelped me, not a brick
>   remains
> of the tenement I reached the age of reason in. Whole
> streets are remade, the cranes erect over Eurocrat schemes
> down the docks. There is nothing
> to show you there, not a trace of a girl
>
> in ankle socks and hand-me-downs sulking (*PT* 14)

In this poem, space has become so deeply invested with meaning that the city streets become the narrator's true home, the literal source of a rangy, animal self now violated by developers. But the poem transforms the loss of these old streets through sexual play, place reclaimed as the private act is described in public terms:

> Climb in here between the sheets
> in the last light of the April evening. We'll trust
> the charts of our bodies. They've brought us
> safe to each other, battle-scarred and frayed
> at the folds, they'll guide us to many wonders.
> Come, let's play in the back streets and tidal flats
> til we fall off the edge of the known world,
>
> and drown. (*PT* 15)

Here nature is an embodied relation beyond the binaries of city and country. The narrator consciously surrenders to the body with its animal wisdom, which can be trusted to lead her and her lover through literal and emotional landscapes, all of them in flux. A boundary-crossing streetwalker, she returns us to the figure of the shape-shifter whose powers of transformation continually re-establish the intimate connections between the human and the nonhuman.

POET AS SHAPE-SHIFTER

The shape-shifter's extraordinary identification with a numinous animal world is part of what draws Meehan, who sees this practice as active in daily life:

> I think people shape-shift all the time. It's a natural thing. I know I do it walking through different areas. If I'm in a rough part of New York, I walk like those around me. We need protective coloring. The animal part of us . . . the more we trust that part of us, the more safe we are. (O'Halloran and Maloy 13)

For Meehan, then, shape-shifting is an active practice acknowledging the wilderness within: collapsing the boundaries between human and animal, she celebrates a deep instinctual knowing, retrieving a premodern belief in the efficacy of living with more than one skin.

In her 1999 interview with Danielle Sered, Meehan describes how an early encounter with the work of American poet Gary Snyder, particularly his undergraduate thesis on a shape-shifting myth of the Haida Indians, a Native tribe of the North American Northwest Coast culture, led her to the oral narratives of her own culture's Bronze Age. Snyder describes shape-shifting myths as central to cultures that grant animals equal status with humans, "just like people, only living in different skins": "The Haida believed both animals and people had souls, which were essentially the same. The bodies of different animals were merely their "canoes" and all were capable of assuming other forms at will; or better, they possessed a human form, and assumed their other forms when consorting with men" (Dimensions 38). Snyder suggests that for the Haida animals are always able to assume human form, but not all humans have the capacity to shape-shift. And animals usually prefer to appear to humans in their nonhuman skins, perhaps because when they do appear as humans, the uninitiated humans often hide these skins, forcing them to curtail their boundary crossing and remain in the human realm.

This refusal of the ambiguous status of the shape-shifter and the intimate connections between the human and nonhuman that shape-shifters represent appear in Meehan's "Island Burial." The poem opens with a headnote that tells us, "They bury their dead as quickly as they can before the shapechanging shames them and gets them branded as witches" (*PT* 64). In the poem, what cannot be hidden is a dead daughter's return to her animal skin, a hare. Though the transformation shames and endangers the family, clearly what is demonized and marginalized by the community is the human body's commonality with all living creatures, the mutable nature of bodies, the inevitability of death. Perhaps for this reason, the grave's is the first voice we hear in the poem: "I am the grave waiting / patient receptive damp / for my hare girl in flux" (*PT* 61). Indeed, the grave is the only speaker in the poem who fully acknowledges, accepts, and even cherishes the daughter's true mortal nature, caught in the flux of shape-shifting from girl to hare, "flesh to dust." The other voices in the poem are both communal and indirect, the graveside prayer and the children's riddle and rhyme about witches and hares. By representing the earth as both final resting place and the poem's only active agent, "Island Burial" reminds us of the indominable aspects of nature: ultimately humans can only witness and participate in the cycles of life and death, praying and puzzling over the mystery.

For those who actively embrace such mysteries, the figure of the shape-shifter becomes an emblem from premodern cultures worth retrieving. The permeable boundaries between humans and animals are, for Miranda and Stephen Green, most easily crossed from the human realm by the shaman, who is often accompanied by an animal helper, and "whose liminal state between earthworld and the domain of the spirits shows itself in terms of an unstable, unfixed identity" (205). For Gary Snyder, both the shamanic trance and poetic inspiration grant access to the "systems of symbolic fantasy" (Snyder, *Myths and Texts* viii) present in the psyche of any individual in a given society. Thus, both shaman and poet play important roles in constructing cultural myths informed by and informing the cultures of which they are a part.

Meehan has often spoken of Snyder's influence on Irish poets of her generation, and her descriptions of poetry as a vocation are clearly informed by his work. Encouraged by the example of poet Michael Harnett to read and listen to the Irish language again, she observes the ways her own poetry comes in part from her "studies of tribal societies":

> The materials I work with are from the oral tradition and they are spoken artifacts rather than written artifacts. The book is the record of the voice rather than the other way around. . . . So in my task of imaginary reconstructions of a tribal past I imagine what the poets must have been, what their function was in their culture and I don't know if it has changed very much. (Praga 74)

At home with hybridity, duality, and the border crossing between a dominant culture's constructed binaries, Meehan along with Snyder retrieves, in Raymond Williams's terms, "the residual," picking up an occulted cultural strand and incorporating it into her poetic practice as part of a communal mission. An element of the past active in the present, the residual, for Williams, is not fully acknowledged by the dominant culture because it is a potential threat to the story of reality that culture is trying to tell:

> Certain experiences, meanings, and values which cannot be expressed or substantially verified in terms of the dominant culture, are nevertheless lived and practiced on the basis of the residue . . . of some previous social and cultural institution or formation. It is

crucial to distinguish this aspect of the residual, which *may have an alternative or even oppositional relation to the dominant culture.* (*Marxism and Literature* 122; emphasis added)

For Williams, although the dominant culture attempts to diffuse the threat of the residual by partly incorporating it, through "re-interpretation, dilution, projection, discriminating inclusion and exclusion" (*Marxism and Literature* 123), literature can actively sustain residual meanings and values in the face of pressure for incorporation.

I want to suggest, then, that Meehan's critical ecofeminist poetics recuperates a shamanic role for the contemporary poet. Consummate shape-shifter, the shamanic poet makes her home in liminality and offers a vision of a re-enchanted world with human and nonhuman in intimate dialogue. Indeed, Meehan describes the writing of poetry in language that suggests the fluid boundaries of the ego characteristic of both shamanic trance and Buddhist meditation, the latter most fully explored in *Dharmakaya*. Thus, shape-shifting becomes a metaphor for the "ability of art to shape and change the self" precisely by allowing the poet to slip between the boundaries of fixed identities. As Meehan describes the process, "I don't use a trustworthy *I* in the poetry. . . . I'm playing all the time with *I* because I don't have an identity. . . . Part of the game in poetry is playing with that transformative *I*" (Sered). For Meehan the poem charts the process of shape-shifting, the ground covered by this transformative *I*, becoming a kind of map left for others: "I would find poetry a certain set of instructions to get through difficult terrain" (Sered). This view of the poet returns her to a fully communal role, one that Victor Turner acknowledges in his study of initiation rites and passage rituals. Shedding light on the generative role of liminal periods and liminal figures in established cultures, Turner observes, "As members of a society, most of us see only what we expect to see, and what we expect to see is what we are conditioned to see when we have learned the definitions and classifications of our culture" (95). But the ambiguity and paradox of liminal experiences and the figures who are witnesses to them disturb established structures and make possible new thoughts and practices: "Liminality may perhaps be regarded as the Nay to all positive structural assertions, but as in some sense the source of them all, and more than that, as a realm of pure possibility whence novel configurations of ideas and relations may arise" (97). In these terms, the poet's willingness to experience and even cultivate liminality by actively crossing boundaries and making a home in inner and outer borderlands becomes one way of re-visioning social worlds.

LIFE IN THE BALANCE

In the winter of 2007, I wrote and revised an early version of this chapter in the infusion room of our local cancer center. I was being treated for breast cancer with Adriamycin, a drug with side effects so fearsome its nickname is the Red Devil. Usually a thorough gatherer of data and an avid questioner, I didn't finish the long list of possible consequences for exposing my body to this drug. My diagnosis didn't allow for many choices.

Instead, I relied on the matter-of-fact kindness of the nurses as they drew my blood for the cell count, inserted the line for the infusion through the port in my chest. In our hushed community of illness, I sat in the row of brown recliners watching the flitting goldfinches at feeders outside the long windows. And tethered to the IV bag, sometimes with a pale blue curtain drawn, I worked. I put down the lines, accumulated the pages.

What I see in the writing now is my desire to take the full measure of Meehan's work before she made the transformative leap into the poems of *Dharmakaya*. I wanted to retrace those origins and the ardor of that process. Midlife turning points take many forms, and I was in the middle of my own fraught passage. There is something boundaryless and unflinching in the essay as I met Meehan's poems and they met me. Liminality. Rites of passage. Shamanic shape-shifting. These poems moved with me between worlds.

And so, the essay emerged with my life in the balance. An in-betweenness marked its progress. I had heard from Meehan herself for the first time in mid-February when I was midway through the Red Devil treatments, midway through the drafting. She had written to thank me for my care with her poems in an essay I'd published a year earlier. She couldn't have known how thoroughly her poems were now caring for me.

* * *

In the winter of 2002 I read my first academic paper on Meehan's work to a small audience in the north Georgia mountains. It was the Southern Regional meeting of the American Conference for Irish Studies at Young Harris College. Moved by the courage and power of "The View from Under the Table" and "Fist" in *Dharmakaya*, I returned to my room after the presentation with a new kind of courage and wrote the draft of what became "First Mammogram."

First Mammogram

Whoever built this machine
couldn't love breasts.

I am between glass plates
and no one has performed the ritual
of asking the body's forgiveness:
For the pain you are about to receive

Instead, it's like the way
we slaughter animals.

When the nurse says they've found
a mass, my knees buckle.
We are strangers beneath bright lights.

Sonogram. Ultrasound. This room is darker
but I'm not convinced it's for me
the lights are dimmed. Then I wait

for another stranger, a man
who has seen inside the soft tissue:
probably a scar in only 1% of such cases
does it turn out to be I am safe for the time
being as I'll ever be unless it changes
in six months we'll see you again

I might have told him
this is where the belt buckle
marked me when I was fourteen

or I know a man is dangerous
when I dream a woman with
a scar on her chest, female Parzival
in a wasteland.
But no one here wants to hear
and I don't remember myself

until later, with my clothes on
when I recall my young breast
with a scar like a brand
my father made
I had not thought so deep.
        (Kirkpatrick *Fisher Queen* 81)

How does embodied experience inform our work as literary and
cultural critics? Then how does the work we make in turn transform us? The poem critiques a masculinized medical system and
couples the female body with the degraded lives of other animals.
Here, too, are marks of the infrequent but significant eruptions
of violence in my childhood home, along with the impact on the

health of a daughter who figures herself as a warrior in a ruined landscape.

I'm struck now by the poem's awareness of the quest through illness and insight I was going to make. A patriarchal culture was the larger source of the wounding, the female body sustaining microaggressions even in attempting to preserve health. Sacrifice. Slaughtered animals. The illness would ultimately leave me without a breast, and knowing so fully my own animal body, soon after I lost the desire to eat the bodies of other animals.

What I knew I admired about Meehan's poems was the wider frame they gave to personal suffering, the historical depth and context. I found I needed myth, history, and feminism but also materialist analysis, Marx on social class. That framing and grounding gave an anchor. It was a way of being in one's life that did not accept the reduced terms of a dominant culture. It was a way of deciding for oneself what one had lived and why. I wanted a vision rooted not in victims, sacrifice, and tragedy but in understanding in the widest sense. Meehan had transformed the materials of her life, and I could too. It was like stepping out of the slow violence of our class status and seeing it, really seeing it.

3

TOWARD AN ANIMISTIC VISION

———

Meehan's perspective powerfully addresses our historical moment of social and environmental crisis, when a change of consciousness and a shift in paradigm require intelligent retrievals and artful appropriations of alternative cosmologies. Just as U.S. poet Gary Snyder's work both draws on and extends influences beyond national boundaries, Meehan's poems, as we have seen, reflect a border-crossing sensibility informed by a working-class Dublin childhood and a keen understanding of the multiple dispossessions made possible by colonialism's current manifestation as corporate globalization. For these reasons, Meehan's distance from dominant discourses of gender, class, and nature may be greater than that of many of her readers and her proximity to counternarratives generative of the cultural work her poems perform. Mindful of Gayatri Spivak's formulation "strategic essentialism" (*In a Word* 116), I propose that Meehan's poetry engages in a "strategic animism" whereby a knowing subject enacts re-engagements with efficacious belief systems from the past. By retrieving animals and plants from the margins, Meehan's narrators reopen a dialogue with an animate nonhuman realm still embraced by Indigenous cultures. Moreover, in *Painting Rain* (2009), Meehan recuperates elements of ancient tree worship to explore human interdependencies with the plant world.

Gary Snyder's oeuvre, which is central to the development of Meehan's poetics and politics, has long included, among its many celebrations of the living nonhuman realm, hymns to trees. His early collection, *Myths and Texts* (1978), opens with a dirge for logged forests around the world, written in the rhythms "of long days of quiet in lookout cabins; setting chokers for the Warm Springs Lumber Co. (looping cables on logs and hooking them to D8 Caterpillars—dragging and rumbling through the brush); and the songs and dances of Great Basin Indian tribes I used to hang around" (vii). This willingness to inhabit the borderlands of a dominant culture while bearing witness to its myriad abuses of what Winona LaDuke has called "all our relations," "animals, fish, trees, and rocks" (2), is common to both Snyder's and Meehan's writing. And both poets call on alternative cosmologies and spiritual traditions to suggest that the violation of our nonhuman relations is of a piece with violence toward human Others. Snyder closes his sequence "Logging" in *Myths and Texts* with a shocking stanza linking the destruction of sacred groves throughout human history with the cutting down of human lives: "Sawmill temples of Jehovah. / Squat black burners 100 feet high / Sending the smoke of our burnt / Live sap and leaf / To his eager nose" (15). A Judeo-Christian god party to the leveling of pagan groves is also complicit with death camps; the destruction of living trees and human beings are so intertwined that they go up in smoke together.

When Snyder entered the lives of Meehan's generation of Irish poets in the 1970s, his disaffection with the values of the U.S. settler culture described in *Myths and Texts*—"a still rootless population of non-natives who don't even know the plants or where our water comes from" (viii)—spoke to a postcolonial and class anger in Dublin's own youth culture. Countering the cultural toxins of colonial mentality, class prejudice, and gender stereotypes, "the ideas coming in through poetry like Snyder's . . . were giving me an alternative to what I was getting through the church, the state, and the family," Meehan has observed. "And certainly that opening out and that influence has lasted up to this day" (Allen Randolph, "Body Politic" 248). Snyder condemns the colonial history of his own country and renames the United States "Occupied Turtle

Island" (Myths & Texts viii). His work charts a quest "to actually 'belong to the land'" (Myths & Texts viii) by resisting a narrative of conquest. A lifelong student of both American Indian cosmologies and Zen Buddhism, Snyder has used these oppositional discourses and practices to reforge his relation to a particular place over the last forty years, a home called Kitkitdizze—named for a local plant—in the foothills of the Sierra Nevada. By integrating Indigenous belief systems, not only has Snyder become a model for doing "the work of becoming who you are, where you are" (*Real Work* 16), he has also served as an important transmitter of alternative worldviews to Western readers and writers. For Meehan, his writing remains an important source: "One of the first contemporary poetry books I held in my hands was Gary Snyder's *Regarding Wave*, back in the seventies. I still read Snyder on a daily basis" (Sperry, "An Interview").

This engagement with Snyder's work, and through him with Buddhist and American Indian views of nature as animate, informs Meehan's complex view of "the interpenetration of all species and all creatures on the planet" (Allen Randolph, "Body Politic" 249). An early instance appears in the title poem of her second collection, *Reading the Sky* (1986), where the narrator turns the comfortably modernist notion of looking for weather patterns on its head by gathering omens from "the cyphers the wild geese drew // Across the violet sky" (*RS* 13). Here, in dialogue with the narrator, the nonhuman participates in its own naming, becoming a source of new human knowledge: "We measured the angles of the stars / Revealed by the dwindling light / And gave to them new names // Learned from the geese in flight" (*RS* 13). Moreover, the reciprocal encounter with birds and sky supplies the narrator and her companion with "a common language" of interconnection to name their own futures, "to describe our differing fates" (*RS* 13). This animistic view of the natural world contains the human-made in the poem that follows, "Chapman Lake: Still Life with Bomber," where the narrator's holiday beside a lake includes a U.S. war plane as another aspect of the landscape: "The B52 bomber roars over. /

It is as much a part of this lake / As those pines, those flies. / It too has designed its part / In my casual holiday. // Pines, bomber, flies, lake" (*RS* 15). The gleaner of omens includes the human-made among her symbols, erasing the boundaries between nature and culture by leveling any hierarchy between them. The binaries continue to collapse as machine emerges animate, capable of its own unsettling designs. Indeed, the ironic echoing of Yeats's line from "Easter 1916," "He, too, has resigned his part / In the casual comedy," in Meehan's "It too has designed its part / In my casual holiday" substitutes "bomber" for "MacBride," suggesting both are "drunken, vainglorious lout[s]." Set on U.S. soil and employing an emblem of imperialism, this poem, among many others, aligns Meehan's work with Snyder's own dissenting poetics.

Central to that poetics is Snyder's "basic perception of animism," "that on one level there is no hierarchy of qualities in life—that the life of a stone or a weed is as completely beautiful and authentic, wise and valuable as the life of, say, an Einstein" (*Real Work* 17). This radical democratization among humans and nonhumans appears everywhere in Snyder's writing, the language of landscape sometimes intermingled with images of the human body as in "Straight-Creek-Great Basin," where "Creek boulders show the flow-wear lines / in shapes the same / as running blood / carves in the heart's main / valve" (*Turtle* 52). Calling at the close of *Turtle Island* for the democratic representation of all life forms in any humane and sustainable society (1974), Snyder grants trees the status of "people of the land" because they "do the primary energy transformation that makes all the life-forms possible. . . . So perhaps plant-life is what the ancients meant by the great goddess" (108).

Such artful appropriations of premodern discourses for a postmodern culture connect both Snyder's and Meehan's work with a powerful ecopolitics. Indeed, for socialist ecofeminists like Vandana Shiva, Indigenous peoples of the world provide us with the best models for conservation because their cultural practices are informed by the values of biodiversity; animistic belief systems grant all life-forms "an inherent right to life": "Sacred groves, sacred seeds, and sacred species have been the cultural means for treating biodiversity as inviolable, and present us with the best examples of conservation" (*Biopiracy* 77). For Shiva, such beliefs should be considered futuristic rather than primitive because their sustainable models also provide powerful ground for resistance. For example, in Chipko, India, the belief in forests as mothers who provide the sustenance of water, food, fuel, fodder, and medicine has empowered Indian women to stop destructive logging and mining of their native forests:

> Throughout the 1970s, in village after village, women would come out and by hugging trees—*chipko* means hug or embrace—prevent the logging companies from destroying their forests. . . . In the act of embracing trees as their kin, ordinary women mobilized an energy more powerful than the police and the brute strength of the logging interests. (*Earth Democracy* 67)

The Chipko women's belief in their kinship with trees is grounded in a direct relationship with the forests as sources of their own lives. Hence, animism involves a deep awareness that human and nonhuman are inextricably interwoven: humans cannot survive and thrive without their nonhuman kin. In these terms, animism as a belief system in which "everything in nature, including what is now considered inanimate, is alive and has an inner spirit, soul, or organizing power" (Merchant, *Columbia Guide* 193) is clearly informed and sustained by a way of life. Thus, when I call Meehan's animism "strategic," I am trying to account for an important self-awareness involved in its deployment: postmodern citizens of Western industrialized societies cannot abandon the experience of modernity for any absolute and uncritical embrace of alternative cosmologies. Yet by "animism" I am suggesting something more than a colorful metaphor, something less than an uncritical embrace. By "strategic" I mean that such a practice of "reading the sky" might serve as one tool among many for knowing one's world. Finally, my use of "strategic animism" attempts to mark the distance a citizen, largely informed by the experience of modernity, must travel to adopt a belief system like animism.

TREES IN *THE GOLDEN BOUGH*

We can see the distance to be traveled in James Frazer's flawed classic, *The Golden Bough* (1922), which gives us a history of tree worship throughout the world from a modern's lofty perspective: "To the savage the world in general is animate, and trees and plants are no exception to the rule. He thinks that they have souls like his own, and he treats them accordingly" (128). Because Frazer is so committed to the virtues of modernity and because he sees the passage from animism to polytheism, for example, as such an unequivocal advance in human cultures, his work suggests what is at stake in both a belief system like animism as well as its abandonment:

> When a tree comes to be viewed, no longer as the body of the tree-spirit, but simply as its abode which it can quit at pleasure, an important advance has been made in religious thought. Animism is passing into polytheism. In other words, instead of regarding each tree as a living and conscious being, man now sees it merely a lifeless, inert mass, tenanted for a longer or shorter time by a supernatural being who, as he can pass freely from tree to tree, thereby enjoys a certain right of possession or lordship over the trees, and ceasing to be a tree-soul, becomes a forest-god. (135–36)

From a tree with a soul to a god of trees: here a forest-god, increasingly in the likeness of a human, has dominion over the trees and forest rather than being bound by them, one survival depending upon the other. Moreover, because the tree has become "a lifeless, inert mass," it is merely of use, without rights or protection. It is a short step to Snyder's loggers. What is lost emerges in Frazer's record of the Missouri Indians, for example, who felt such empathy for the suffering of trees that they believed when one was swept away by a flooded current, "the spirit of the tree cries, while the roots still cling to the land" (129). Thus, the Missouri considered it wrong to fell trees, and "when large logs were needed, they made use only of trees which had fallen themselves" (129).

Common in tree worship is the belief that the souls of the dead inhabit them. "Among the Igorrotes, every village has its sacred tree, in which the souls of the dead forefathers of the hamlet reside. Offerings are made to the tree, and any injury done to it is believed to entail some misfortune on the village. Were the tree cut down the village and all its inhabitants would inevitably perish" (Frazer 133). Frazer describes trees in China planted on the graves of the dead "in order to thereby strengthen the soul of the deceased and thus to save his body from corruption" (133); in this case, the dead are literally incorporated into the body of the tree. This shape-shifting between human and nonhuman tree suggests an important ethic among Buddhists familiar in both Snyder's and Meehan's writing: believing "that to destroy anything whatever is forcibly to dispossess a soul, [Buddhists] will not break a branch of a tree as they will not break the arm of an innocent person" (Frazer 129). Drawing on elements of animistic tree worship, Meehan's sequence of poems, "A Change of Life," in *Painting Rain* (2009), gives us access to what it might mean for postmodern citizens to live *as if* kin to trees.

"WHAT YOU SHOULD KNOW TO BE A POET"
"A Change of Life" takes as its epigraph the last line of what Meehan has suggested is one of her founding texts, Snyder's "What You Should Know to Be a Poet," from his early collection, *Regarding Wave* (1970). Snyder's is a poem of instruction written as an informal list for the prospective poet. Its injunctions largely bypass human literary traditions in favor of a deep knowledge of the fauna and flora of place as tools for developing the intuitive and instinctual. Indeed, we might read "What You Should Know to Be a Poet" as a rendering in verse of Snyder's early description of

poet as shaman, retrieving "the most archaic values on earth" from the "upper Palaeolithic." These values include "the fertility of the soil, the magic of animals, the power-vision in solitude, the terrifying initiation and rebirth, the love and ecstasy of the dance, the common work of the tribe" (*Myths* viii). Meehan recalls her early encounter with this poem: "luckily Snyder was a poet working in the wisdom tradition, so you could actually take it literally and not get into too much danger. . . . I wouldn't have taken that poem metaphorically, I would have taken it as real" (Allen Randolph, "Body Politic" 247). And it is precisely a reframing of the real that Snyder's poem asks the neophyte poet to know: "all you can about animals as persons. / the names of trees and flowers and weeds. / names of stars, and the movements of the planets and the moon" (*Regarding Wave* 40). If, like Meehan, we take these "injunctions literally," we find ourselves in the presence of an organismic view of nature where animals are helpers and kin; plants and planets have proper names; knowledge of both the visible and unseen, the natural and supernatural, is accessed both empirically and intuitively; and a poet's texts include the material world, the dream world, and the illusory world of the psyche's projections. This late-twentieth-century reframing of the mechanistic model of nature connects Meehan through Snyder with the tradition of nineteenth-century Romanticism, which Carolyn Merchant has described as a "turning back to the organismic idea of a vital animating principle binding together the whole created world" (*Death of Nature* 100). In this context, belief in a radical interpenetration not only of all creatures and species but of the entire world, natural and supernatural, makes Snyder's injunction that the poet know "at least one kind of traditional magic" consistent with this organismic worldview—though the admission of a plurality of approaches in "at least one kind" provides a postmodern update. As in Meehan's early poem, "Reading the Sky," geese might indeed provide omens if they are interwoven with a larger whole, sharing a common language of interconnection. And the tools of magic and divination might grant, at the very least, intuitive access to "a vast organism, everywhere quick and vital, its body, soul, and spirit . . . held tightly together" (Merchant, *Death of Nature* 104).

Aptly, Meehan has described Snyder's poem as "an opening out into a perception of a world where there could be integration" (Allen Randolph, "Body Politic" 247). In "A Change of Life," the narrator takes up Snyder's injunctions, the sequence opening with a ritual prayer before the commencement of a journey, and the narrator taking her cue from elements in the natural world—"that raindrop / on the tip of a tansy leaf" (*PR* 62)—that serve as able guides. Though an earlier sequence about trees, "Six Sycamores," features a figure in the section called "Liminal," who has found "a clear path through the chaos," where "nothing can harm" or "cure," the narrator in "A Change of Life" is more concerned with staying the course in a city that threatens to kill her with grief. The charge is made more difficult by the speaker's own vulnerable transitional status, "a change of life" echoing "the change of life" even as it suggests the *I Ching* counseled in Snyder's poem, a divination tool that might help to show the way. Rather than the delight in "thresholds, the stepping over, / the shapechanging that can happen when / you jump off the edge into pure breath" sung by the speaker of "Liminal," the narrator of "A Change of Life" prays for something akin to the former speaker's poise and longs for a return, for a "green wave" that might "break over my ageing body" (*PR* 63).

Here is a poem of major transformation at midlife when the role of communal witness requires all the poet's strength. The speaker knows much of the terrain, giving her own injunctions and well aware of the process she's to endure: "Elemental now, or mental / my two feet solid on this earth—/ the path ahead, the path behind" (*PR* 62). The wry play of "mental" and "elemental" evokes the ritual stripping and debasement of initiation ceremonies, the old self ground down for the new. Yet even with "two feet solid on this earth," what haunts the narrator is precisely the puzzle of place. The "question of when to move" in "The Book of Changes" calls to the "repotting" in "Solomon's Seal" and to that section's rest-less "will I still live in this suburban estate / when the mystery of the seal breaks open" (*PR* 63). The challenge of belonging to a par-ticularly conflicted place emerges again in "Sweeping the Garden" with a discounted gypsy child swept from Irish culture, given by her teacher the "blunt tool" of an out-of-date calendar, which the child has humor and wit enough to interpret: "I'm living in the past!" (*PR* 64). Ironically, the narrator, engaged herself in pre-modern ways of knowing, works to educate a child, "traveler still, forever gypsy," into modernity though her student already pos-sesses a "beautiful cultured mind": "She swims in the oral: look-ing into a written sentence / is like looking into a bush. Numbers / are blackbirds that all flap up together from the page" (*PR* 64). The child needs the tools of modernity to function in a postmodern capitalist culture, although that culture resigns her to a lowly class status with "each and every long-drawn / incarcerated moment of her school year" (*PR* 64).

Central to "A Change of Life" is a dying chestnut grove. The trees make their first appearance in the third section of the poem where they are coupled with a demented youth exposing himself outside a train station. Entitled "Scrying," this poem gestures back to "The Book of Changes," both sections alluding to Snyder's "What You Should Know to Be a Poet" as well as pre-dicting the future of a New Ireland for those left behind. Here the whole island is caught up in and controlled by the shadows of money and power, desire unleashed in an excess that amounts to surrender to the more base instincts out of balance: "wander-ing around with our lower material selves / hanging out—like that boy the other day // near the dying chestnuts at the station / who, shaking his penis at me, screamed / *What are you looking at, witch?*" (*PR* 63). The proximity of the boy's distorted sexu-ality to the dying chestnuts suggests the counter-generative ex-cesses of the New Ireland. This is not Snyder's wilderness on the San Juan Ridge in the Yuba River watershed but a Dublin housing estate with its entrenched class politics exacerbated by the worsening inequities of a Tiger economy. What the poet sees and continues to see "breaks my heart" (*PR* 64). As if to underline the toxicity of this environment for human and non-human alike, the boy lashes out in the poem's concluding line, aggressively complicit with the cultural forces inimical to him as well. Narrator and reader shoulder the intended slur of *witch*, which accurately registers a dominant culture's assessment of the worldview the poem offers.

The poet's immersion in the demonic aspects of her own culture in "Scrying" finds its counterpart in the second half of Snyder's "What You Should Know to Be a Poet," where the poem moves to an archetypal realm in which Snyder's narrator encounters both "devil" and "hag" and is enjoined to "fuck" them both. In Jungian terms, this call to struggle with both the unintegrated shadow side of the self and the darkest forces in nature, including human nature, hones the poet for genuine relations with human lovers and friends. What's left after these mythic transformations is an alert engagement with the mundane: immersion in the ephemeral oddities of one's own popular culture, including "children's games, comic books, bubble-gum, / the weirdness of television and advertising" (*Wave* 40) as well as patient acceptance of work, the work of craft and basic human labor for sustenance.

But the apparent innocence of "children's games, comic books, and bubble-gum" in Snyder's poem is lost for the working-class children in the fifth section of Meehan's sequence. The demented boy of "Scrying" finds his double "where the boy racer has hit the wall—/ *Coked up to the gills*, says the cop" (*PR* 65). The title, "Common Sense," emerges as the necessary counterpart to divination, the poem opening with a tree said to protect against witches, the rowan. But as if to suggest that common sense need not trump animistic belief but might instead exist strategically alongside it, the rowan does not repel this postmodern witch. Rather, the harvest of a "mid-August berry feast" rains down on her head, aligning her, if unceremoniously, with pagan celebrations of seasons.

Here is a tree fulfilling its role of kinship, supplying the narrator with abundance. It serves as counterpoint to the dying chestnut grove where children gathered up into poverty and ignorant of the trees that provide them with the pleasures of conkers strip the bark from the source that nurtures them. These are misguided tree worshippers: "their rapt gazes as they stript / might have lent a Renaissance artist faces for an altarpiece" (*PR* 65). Their fates inextricably bound with the trees they injure, the children cannot be saved by a narrator who refrains from dealing the cards that spell "bad luck / in store for them down their roads" (*PR* 65). And neither can she save the trees, though the poem suggests what might have:

> I wanted to wrap the trees in woolly jumpers—
> those saplings shivering through the winter.
> I watched them fail to bud and fail to leaf.
>
> I watched them die through fair weather
> through foul I have watched them die.
> My beloved young chestnut grove.
> And now an autumn without conkers! (*PR* 65)

The narrator's longing to embrace the trees as kin emerges not only in the image of "woolly jumpers" but also in the eulogy the poem provides, its perfect iambic pentameter line—"I watched them fail to bud and fail to leaf "—in poignant lyric counterpoint to a lost spring. Interdependent with the community, the trees cannot survive without knowledgeable caretakers, and their loss deprives the neighborhood of one of its seasonal pleasures. With "My beloved young chestnut grove," Meehan's narrator evokes sacred groves and a way of life that sustained them. Recalling the "oak-worship of the Druids," Frazer found among the Celts the word for *sanctuary* "identical in origin and meaning with the Latin *neums*, a grove or *woodland*" (127). Without the sanctuary the trees provide, "Common sense dictates there'll be bad luck" (*PR* 65): humans cannot thrive without their nonhuman kin.

A volume of eulogies interlinking human and nonhuman destinies, *Painting Rain* mourns the deaths of fields and trees alongside the deaths of friends and family. Indeed, we might find in the burying of these dead another form of tree worship, lives memorialized in poems and incorporated into the paper of a book, which was once the wood of trees. "A Change of Life" concludes with one such memorial for a cousin raised as a sister, mourned in the presence of leaf, rain, and flower. In "Hectic" the body of Paula McCarthy becomes the body of the tree as the narrator lets go: "I'll let you drop leaf by leaf into the void" (*PR* 66). Trees and departed sister merge again in the image of "the trees hectic in the woods," the feverish activity of the grove evoking McCarthy's death by fire. The poem returns us to *Painting Rain*'s opening epigraphs, both Theo Dorgan's "The mysteries of the forest disappear with the forest" and the tail-swallowing wisdom of *The Diamond Sutra*. This Buddhist text, said to compress all teachings into one, takes the image of the diamond to cut through every illusion. Indeed, Meehan's poem suggests that to bear the grief of this much loss requires the hardest transformation, the compassion on the other side of every discarded illusory attachment, the "cut diamond" that might "Spark my obdurate heart" (*PR* 67).

Snyder's "What You Must Know to Be a Poet" concludes by wishing the poet both the eternalized delights of "extasy" in the "wild freedom of the dance" as well as the internal delights of "enstasy" in "silent solitary illumination" (*Regarding Wave* 40). And then there are the fragments with which Meehan's poem begins: "real danger. gambles. and the edge of death" (*PR* 40). Perhaps in returning to the last line of Snyder's founding text at the opening of her own, Meehan means both to reinscribe vocation while also expanding, revising, and updating the first poem's injunctions. While Snyder's poem reads as ahistorical template, Meehan's "A Change of Life" responds with a particular case study. And while the earlier poem's injunctions seem to hold, Meehan suggests that the stamina required to fulfill them is enormous: "Foot before foot slog up the path" (*PR* 67).

INTERVIEW

....

LIFE ISN'T GOING TO BE THE SAME, JUNE 2020

KATHRYN KIRKPATRICK: I always feel when I'm speaking with you that I just want to talk to you. And I don't really want to do an interview, you know? It's like I have my scholarly head over here, and I know there are these questions I need to ask, and yet I just feel like as a poet and as a human being, I just want to talk to you. There's always that tension.

PAULA MEEHAN: But isn't that what I said to you from the very start—that we should have a conversation? And I believe that the general conversation around poetry has now been pushed to a certain edge. I mean, it's a real moment, isn't it?

KK: It is.

PM: All over. And, you know, it's important to hold to integrity and to hold the line and to be aware that there are a lot of agendas out there. The conversation is so ferocious, but it didn't come from nowhere, and the poets have been making the language to have the conversation for the last, well, you could go very far back. But I know that at this particular moment there is a generation pushing to make the Venn diagram where different kinds of grievance and lack of justice can come together.

KK: In my education, the people that I studied with were Marxist literary scholars, and they always wanted to include the ethical and moral dimensions into the study of literature. It's still frustrating to me when I find those dimensions put in opposition to the aesthetic qualities of poetry because they go together in my mind.

PM: Yes, I understand.

KK: I know that poetry is not a political program, but it's also not only an aesthetic artifact. Lately the main things I've written have been thinking on the page about the pandemic: "Okay, we're getting to this place now where capital is going to have to decide: is it the money or is it the people? Is it the money or is it the lives?" That's just so hard to be living through and to be witnessing. This government could take care of all the people; we could have a basic income right now. We could, and we should. Life in the scale is just being laid really bare, and yet not everybody seems to see that.

PM: Wasn't that Marx saying that?

KK: Yes!

PM: I was taught classical history, ancient history, especially of Sparta and Athens, by Paul Cartledge, who was a young lecturer, a recent graduate, and he was basically using a Marxist dialectic to teach ancient history. He was the cutting edge back in the early seventies, in an otherwise quite eccentric and traditional School of Classics in Trinity College Dublin. I was just gone seventeen and I loved both approaches, the radical and the traditional. I felt they balanced each other. Paul Cartledge taught us ancient history completely through the history of the slaves. And W. B. Stanford, the eminent classics scholar and a poet himself, taught us Greek myth and Classical drama. The two approaches have been foundational for my later work in poetry, lenses I use to this day.

KK: Wow.

PM: It's very much about the lens you bring to the world and its past because Paul Cartledge, through giving us that lens to look at that beauty, also developed in us a kind of a heart empathy. We had to take account of the reality that the beauties of the classical world, the archaeological wonders we pored over in the museums and at the sites, were deeply dependent on the sweat of slaves, humans who were owned and traded, and who had no votes or say in the political affairs of what we were being taught was the birthplace of democracy.

That lens was so useful. Paul Cartledge became a preeminent expert on Sparta, and he does a lot of television programs on Sparta and other aspects of the ancient world.

He's a wonderful guide. So you know there's the process of our young ideologies moving through the body into who we are now. I'm well into my third age, and I intend to knock a bit of fun out of it, even if it is during the apocalypse. But all those ideologies—Marxism, different waves of feminism, different waves of socialism and anarchism, all the different kinds of psychedelia, just a fantastic sphere of ideas that I was steeped in during my young intellectual life—it isn't enough to passively experience them. Unless they can process through the body and community, then, you know, they just remain interesting notions. There are times when the conversation becomes really serious. It's a very serious moment at present, serious for poetry, and whether you're writing to the moment or not, this affects us, sweeping through. It's like the statues coming down, monuments to slave owners, Confederate generals, all that. There are many agendas and people get hurt. So I'm seeing all this going on. And my own private practice is the same one I've always had, an instinct of connected sources, whether in memory or in notebooks, guided by poets I've loved. But I know my life isn't going to remain the same. How could it?

4

RESTORING THE GARDEN

——

In an interview in 2008, Paula Meehan discussed the folk roots of a few of the traditional forms in which she works. She spoke of how certain forms can be traced to what she calls the "songs of the people"—for instance, the villanelle's source in the work-song of Roman slaves and the sonnet's origins in an old Sicilian folk song (Allen Randolph, "Body Politic" 263). Mindful that the sonnet was brought into English by Sir Walter Raleigh and Edmund Spenser, Meehan makes clear in the interview that she understands it to be a form that also carries the karma of soldier poets who put to death the last of the Gaelic bards and conducted the ethnic cleansing of their time. Poets, she suggests, are thus working not only with the rhyme schemes, stress patterns, and syllable counts of a received form but also with its sociohistorical accretions—in the case of the sonnet, with the colonial history of its early makers. This multileveled approach to the art of poetry informs Meehan's poems, old and new.

I have been arguing that addressing her work fully requires an expansive ecocritical frame, one that acknowledges the interconnections between exploitative economic systems, social inequities, and environmental degradation. Meehan's representations of gardens—liminal and mediated spaces between human dwelling and wilderness or cityscape—offer a way to explore these interconnections. As Meehan is an urban poet, one might expect gardens to be at most a quiet subtext in her work. We find instead an acute awareness of the garden as a historical structure and a socially constructed form. Meehan works with the colonial history of gardens and the gender politics of the Christian garden story in order to dismantle the garden as the emblem of empire and bourgeois privilege, as well as a site of oppressive gender relations. In the process—or, rather, because of this process—she clears the way for the poet as seer in the service of community. That community includes as an equal partner the nonhuman living world of nature.

Carolyn Merchant argues in *Reinventing Eden: The Fate of Nature in Western Culture* (2004) that, since the seventeenth century, the recovery of the garden of Eden has been the dominant narrative of the West: "Internalized by Europeans and Americans alike . . . this story has propelled countless efforts by humans to recover Eden by turning wilderness into garden, 'female' nature into civilized society, and indigenous folkways into modern culture. Science, technology, and capitalism have provided the tools, male agency the power and impetus" (2). Informed and legitimated by this narrative, colonial expansion engaged both in reclaiming an earth considered fallen and in redeeming it through human labor: a lost Eden needed human cultivation to restore it (however much that labor might be forced). This worldview also saw a disorderly female nature that needed containment. Thus, the Christian doctrine of the Fall used sexist gender ideologies to justify the improving mission of empire:

> In the 1600s, Europeans and New World colonists began a massive effort to rein-vent the whole earth in the image of the Garden of Eden. Aided by the Christian doctrine of redemption and the inventions of science, technology, and capitalism, the longterm goal of the Recovery project has been to turn the entire earth into a vast cultivated garden. (Merchant, *Reinventing* 20)

Ramóne Soto-Crespo, in the course of discussing the garden books of West Indian writer Jamaica Kincaid, discusses the intertwined histories of horticulture and colonialism as well as "the

motif of the garden as imperial trope" (343). He notes that in imperial chronicles, "the myth of the land as garden was concurrent
with the erasure of the indigenous population and the depletion
of tropical vegetation by deforestation" (348). As imperial powers
competed for floral wealth, the term *gardenesque* emerged in the
1830s to describe the effects of transplanted exotics on English
gardens. Victorian and Edwardian country-house gardens became
an opportunity for the display of taste and wealth, and the cultural
institution of the botanical garden emerged as a money-making
enterprise. The indigenous plants of colonized countries were hy-
bridized, "moved from the category of wild to that of cultivated"
(353), and marketed by the botanical trade. Soto-Crespo observes
that by 1848 London's Kew Gardens "was at the vanguard of
British imperialism," "the center of 'a network of government botanical stations . . . stretching from Jamaica to Singapore to Figi'"
(353). With Swedish botanist Carl Linnaeus's creation of a system
of nomenclature for cataloguing plants, the world's flora could be
possessed through renaming and the Garden of Eden restored at
the heart of the empire. In the process, the native roots of what
have become common garden plants were often effectively severed.
As Soto-Crespo observes, "the European conqueror suffered from
an excessive self-love, which translated into his desire to occupy all
space with his own image" (362).

COLONIAL GARDENS

Histories of Irish gardening are bound up with this colonial narrative. Keith Lamb and Patrick Bowe open their 1995 volume
A History of Gardening in Ireland by quoting naturalist Edward
Lhuyd, who in 1700 recorded "an elegant sort of heath bearing
large thyme-leaves, a spike of fair purple flowers" to describe an
Irish specimen "still preserved in the Natural History Museum in
London" (1). Lamb and Bowe tell us that while the indigenous
maidenhair fern is now grown all over the world, "the Killarney
fern . . . suffered severely from plundering during the fashion for

cultivating ferns in Victorian times" (1). In the foreword to Edward Hyams's *Irish Gardens* (1967), a volume that focuses entirely on the colonial gardens of the Anglo-Irish, Daniel Foley is less oblique:

> Though the Irish have always revealed a love of nature in their poetry, song, stone sculpture, metalcraft, illuminated manuscripts, and, perhaps more especially, in the charming place names of their villages, it remained for those beyond their borders to design and develop most of the notable private gardens that today flourish in Ireland. In the eighteenth century and well into the nineteenth, the English gentry built great houses and created gardens truly worthy of their settings. Rare exotic treasures, gathered by intrepid plant hunters from South American jungles and Asian mountain valleys, rooted and flourished in the wet mild climate of Ireland to an extent not realized elsewhere in the British Isles. (5)

Foley suggests that gardening was somehow an art that the multi-talented, nature-loving Irish missed. Moreover, he represents the colonial elite as holding the earth's wild nature at their disposal, emptied of its Indigenous peoples and freely available for the stocking of Anglo-Irish gardens. Among many such gardens in Ireland, we have Annes Grove in County Cork, acquired by the English Grove family in the seventeenth century; Mount Usher in County Wicklow, acquired by the English Walpoles in 1868; Mount Stewart in County Down, bought by the Marquis of Londonderry in the 1920s. In *Finding Ireland* (2008), Richard Tillinghast describes Mount Stewart as a garden paradise where "old roses stop you in your tracks with their fragrances, which seem to encapsulate some essence of the era when they were first cultivated—when life was, by all accounts, sweeter" (228). These rare old roses bear names like Climbing Lady Hillingdon, raised in 1910; Madame Georges Braunt, 1887; and Alister Stella Gray, 1894 (225). His description of Mount Stewart's Shamrock Garden makes no mention of the large Red Hand of Ulster flowerbed in the paving, once planted with *Iresine herbstii*, which has red leaves—a naked declaration of colonists' hold on the land.

Meehan objects to the trope that figures the garden as a remedy for a fallen world, a space where, in Merchant's description, "human labor would redeem the souls of men and women, while the earthly wilderness would be redeemed through cultivation and domestication" (*Reinventing* 21). She sees neither a fallen human nature in need of redemption nor a natural world in need of human cultivation. Meehan's work offers a counternarrative to the colonial "recovery of Eden" story. When asked by Marie Heaney to contribute to a volume that gathered personally inspiring spiritual models, Meehan chose an anonymous tenth-century Irish Christian text called "The Hermit's Hut." In it, a speaker living in the midst of ash, hazel, blackthorn, rowan, and hawthorn celebrates the many gifts of food the forest provides: "sweet apples, red bog berries, whortleberries," "haws, yew berries, kernels of nuts," "pignuts, wild marjoram, the cresses of the stream—green purity!" (39). "The Hermit's Hut" concludes with the evocative line "A beautiful pine makes music to me, it is not hired"—over which Meehan muses, "Had they worries about the commodification of art back then?" (38).

By providing representations of human relations with nature that are more than cash propositions, Meehan suggests that such joyful interchanges are possible even in the built environments of cities:

> Though I am not a Christian, I identify strongly with its urge to worship, and to be transported by the experience of the natural world. I've felt the same delight in a city square watching a blackbird worrying the rasher rind an office worker has discarded from her lunch. It's more than a hymn to nature—it's a hymn to the enoughness of the experience of being alive and an enactment of the eternal playful song of the self in nature. (38)

"The Hermit's Hut" might seem a prelapsarian vision of nature and a model for the Edenic garden humans might restore, but the text moves beyond the binary that would cast nature as provider of plenty without cultivation and nature in need of human cultivation in order to provide at all. Human hands have made the hut's "two heathery door-posts for support," and "tame swine" mix with "goats, young pigs, wild swine, tall deer" and a "badger's brood." The hermit makes beer and mead even as he gathers blackberries and "the cresses of the stream." Moreover, Meehan updates this complex view of nature with the image of the blackbird in a city square worrying a rasher rind discarded by an office worker. Nature is not presented here as pristine wilderness with humans apart but rather as everywhere and including human experience itself. There are elements here of what Merchant has proposed as a "partnership ethic" of

> nature and humanity as equal, interacting, mutually responsive partners. This ethic combines human actions and nature's actions in a dynamic relationship with each other. Here nature is not created specifically for human use, nor are women and animals seen as helpmates for "man." Rather, human life and biotic life exist in mutual support, reciprocity, and partnership with each other. (*Reinventing* 26)

For Merchant, "gardens could exemplify places in which the practice of gardening is a caretaking of the soil and the life it generates" (26).

FINDING A DIFFERENT EDEN

The first appearance of the garden in Meehan's poems comes early in her first book, *Return and No Blame* (1984), where it is part of a scene of bourgeois privilege. "Southside Party" opens with a series of questions suggesting both the impossibility of owning the natural world and the assumption by the propertied classes that they do:

Whose landscape? Whose trees? Whose sky?
Through the clear pane
The pampered garden looks bored. (*RNB* 16)

The clean window on an overtended garden suggests a superfluity of labor at the disposal of this household—nature managed, contained, and kept at arm's length. These relations with the land are mirrored by the social relations indoors where—as elsewhere in her work—Meehan represents interaction between and with middle-class subjects as alienated and alienating: "Marooned in separate states / the people in the room mutter / stories, butter up each other, / disagree or shut up abruptly" (*RNB* 16). A drunken "he," with eyes "blood veined like leafless / Trees on the sky," is the numbed representative of men who take women as they take the land, his hand visibly groping a girl, making "inroads / To the core of her sweet cherry" (*RNB* 16). A burst of vernacular punctuates the poem's ending as the narrator underscores her difference: the empty pleasures of the party carry on "despite / City vicissitudes / City full of platitudes, / Oh, those city attitudes. / Screw yous!" (*RNB* 16). With "Southside Party," Meehan opens her poetic project with a rejection of these gender and class relations. Notably, she sets her discussion of such relations in close proximity to a garden as private property, a display of wealth and status.

The poem in Meehan's work that first calls specific attention to the garden in the title does not feature a literal garden at all. Instead, "The Garden of the Sleeping Poet" in Meehan's second collection, *Reading the Sky* (1985), engages one of the etymological roots of the word *garden*, *garth*, meaning enclosure. The poem explicitly addresses the garden as metaphor both for entrapment as well as for potential rebellion and resistance. The narrator addresses a dear friend, an older poet enclosed in a mental ward. Harassed by one of his nurses, he seeks protection in the stacked manuscripts around his bed, a "fortress of words" (*RS* 14). The narrator feels trapped by another institution, "an American university": "We're both in institutions now, / let's face it. / Between my prison and yours / stands the need for revolution / and one more emigrant's story / of the shores of Amerikay" (*RS* 20). What has broken the older poet is his role as witness to the displacements and forced migrations of a colonial history, the emigrant narrator now among their number:

> I saw in your eyes the countless leavings,
> The wakes for gorgeous bodies that were young
> Yet dead to those who loved them.
> I saw in your eyes the peculiar strength
> It takes to stay and to bury the dead.
> . . .
> Here on my private frontier I'm haunted
> By ghosts of those who came before me:
> The bewildered women on Ellis Island,
> The muscled men who withered to build
> The Northern Pacific Railroad,
> The lost souls pacing hungry streets
> Paved with other men's gold. (*RS* 21)

This poem frames emigration as another phase of the colonization process, and thus another setting for exploitation. The intended escape has been from one class hierarchy to another, an old poverty to a new. Once comrades on the dole meeting in cheap tea shops, the narrator and her friend had nonetheless felt in their art their own form of Eden: "Poets with a whole world to name / Between us in our hands" (*RS* 21). But the poem closes with poetry's unrealized potential to resist the entrapments the poem names, as the narrator addresses her friend "inviolate behind your banks of poems / Safe in the garden of the sleeping poet / Wandering with sky horses / And moons that flower into suns" (*RS* 22). The imagination has not protected this poet from a harsh reality but rather has become its own reality. The garden as enclosure ultimately traps those who seek shelter within its walls.

Ireland's colonial history also looms large in *Reading the Sky*'s most literal garden poem, "Hunger Strike," in which the starving body of Bobby Sands is represented as reliving Ireland's colonial privations: "In the small cage of your body / You must have remembered / The rude march of history" (*RS* 9). The garden in "Hunger Strike" fails to protect and nourish because the public politics of the state—shaped by fallout from a colonial history—undercut the narrator's will to cultivate it. Overwhelmed by the national tragedy of Sands's hunger strike, the narrator neglects her own sources of nourishment as if in solidarity: "I neglected the garden that season, / Took a desultory spate at the hoe / Now and again. I forgot the insistent / Beauty of seeds" (*RS* 9). Here, as in many of Meehan's poems, the boundaries between public and private life are thoroughly permeable, with the private life absorbed by the larger public narrative. Though the garden provides at least the potential for an awareness of cycles of life and death, beginnings and endings, its "beauty of seeds" "insistent," the narrator is reduced only to an awareness of the linear motion of death. In this poem, one of Meehan's recurring and variously wise old women attempts to rescue the narrator: "An old neighbour woman came over / Once near the end. She brought / Soda bread and home made butter / So yellow it hurt to look at it" (*RS* 10).

Is "the end" here that of Sands, or the narrator? The confused reference echoes the narrator's intense empathetic involvement in Sands's story. For her, too, food, the richness of butter, has become painful. Though the old neighbor tries to bring the narrator back to her own life and duties—"She remarked I was losing weight / And looking through the window asked / Did I feel no shame at the rotting harvest" (*RS* 10)—neither embarrassment nor the offer of a religious relic, "a scapular of a saint / She swore by" (*RS* 10), can salvage the situation. Subsumed by the ongoing consequences of a colonial history and reduced to "puny acts" in the face of Sands's dramatic protest, the narrator as diminished state subject echoes, in her garden context, a needless waste of life.

In these early poems of struggle, the narrators most often seek escape from the garden and all it represents. The escapes that Meehan presents are from the enclosures of gender and class oppressions, into the pleasures of the wild and undomesticated. In "When My Father Was a Young Man," an enabling elder woman and a nurturing father launch the young narrator into her own orbit. Although it might seem as if the grandmother's garden is the site of the young girl's transformation, it is the uncultivated state of that garden from which the narrator is launched, "Nanny's garden / Full of daisies before the first summer mowing" (*RS* 31). Flung into the cosmos, the narrator shape-shifts beyond her father: "Older / Than he, I was Nanny herself waving as I passed / Out of human sight to reach one particular / Orbit around the green sun forever" (*RS* 31). The sonnet's rhyme of "mowing" and "growing" suggests that the garden is not a place to stay: the growing girl had best leave it rather than be cut down by cultivation or domestication. In the same way, in "First Communion" new lovers make their own kind of sacrament on the margins of a church procession, lilacs stolen from a garden lying "limp and bedraggled in clusters" (*RS* 40). In this poem, the garden's offerings are illicit and the worse for wear; pleasure lies outside the garden. The preference is driven home in the short "Postcard from Ithaca," one of many poems in Meehan's work where the beloved is allied to the undomesticated and feral: "The kitchen garden's full with ripening fruit / But the speedwell in the fallow field / Has kept the blue in your eyes" (*RS* 43). In this short poem, cultivated land is sensibly arranged, close to hand and productive. Yet the coordinating conjunction "but" leans toward the "fallow field" where the uncultivated and undomesticated "has kept" what has been lost through cultivation: the landscape's older, original information.

More pointedly, in "Zugzwang," a poem in Meehan's third collection, *The Man Who Was Marked by Winter* (1994), the cultivated garden is rendered as failed domesticity. The poem opens in the medieval and Renaissance manner with flowers as explicit symbols, an anthropocentrism that echoes a male painter's anthrocentric attempts to frame his female companion as a work of art. The evocatively named garden annual with crimson tassels known as love-lies-bleeding becomes "a token of domestic tragedy, a wound";

similarly, the female lover in the poem is also recast by the assessing eye of the painter as a figure from "Dutch paintings, bourgeois / interiors, *Woman Washing, Woman Setting / a Table / Woman Bending Over a Child*" (*MMW* 14). Yet, despite the male lover's attempts to contain her in "a painting half-made—*Woman Surrounded by Flowers at a Sink*" (*MMW* 12). the female figure in the poem lurches out of the domestic frame, a departure with a high cost, as the title of the poem suggests. Zugzwang is a chess term for the situation of a player who cannot move without disadvantage. Confined in the domestic enclosure figured by the garden, the female lover suffers both from the containment and from her efforts to extricate herself. The interior of her house is haunted by her own mother's disappointments in marriage, as when she hears "her dead mother's voice / tumbling in the dryer with the wash: *I told you so, I told you so, I told you so*" (*MMW* 15). Outdoors, cultivated space is likewise mixed up with this inherited script of domestic trauma. The garden is the site of a half-crazed acting out as the woman digs in the night rain for her dead:

> He found her
> digging in the garden, her nightgown
> drenched through, muck smeared on her arms,
> on her legs, the rain lashing down.
> She explained that she wanted to be close
> to her loved ones, her lost ones, that
> they are so cold and lonely in the earth
> and they long for the warmth of the living. (*MMW* 15)

In this scene, a premodern relation to the land is enacted, albeit in distorted form: the garden here is imagined as sacred site of the dead ancestors. "Zugzwang" represents an instinct to search for alternatives to the modern bourgeois marriage by turning again to what Raymond Williams has called "residual" elements of the past (*Marxism and Literature* 122).

In this sense, Meehan's poem also suggests a loss of context for the modern romantic relationship. The larger nexus of communal relations is restored disturbingly in the poem through a mother's haunting voice and the claims of the ancestral dead on the living. Yet these connections between marriage and community, between marriage and the land, in Williams's terms, "cannot be expressed or substantially verified in terms of the dominant culture" (*Marxism and Literature* 122). Instead, the attempt to resist the insularity of the modern bourgeois marriage appears in the poem in the only way modernity allows: as madness. Hence, in "Zugzwang," the woman's attempts to resist the oppressions of bourgeois domesticity results in a "shatter into smithereens" (16). The male artist will refigure her according to his own premodern vision as "a priestess in a Minoan rite, / devotee of the bull, and himself a mosaic worker / fingering a thousand fragments until he finds / the exact shade of blue with that green undertow / to fit his pattern" (*MMW* 15). The poem concludes with a shard of the fragmented woman reflecting "her beloved sky beyond / like a calm ocean lapping at the mountain" (*MMW* 16). The image of an unbounded natural world—beyond the garden and its socially constructed frames—suggests the broader movement of Meehan's poems toward ecocentric relations with the land that can, in turn, give rise to more liberatory relations between men and women.

Given Meehan's rendering of the garden as itself a fallen place, the site of failed gender relations and colonial reverberations, it is not surprising that we find narrators abandoning the garden in all its conventional forms in her next collection, *Pillow Talk* (1994). Indeed, in "Not alone the rue in my herb garden," a poem located near the center of this collection, a narrator revisits the domestic enclosure she has left behind, "abandoned gardens, abandoned husband, / abandoned cat and dog and chickens, / abandoned quilts and embroideries" (*PT* 44). This speaker recalls the cultivated garden and the bourgeois marriage as joyless struggle, in which transformations of the land and of the self were hard-won:

"We built this soil together, husband; / barrow after barrow load of peat / sieved through an old chop strainer / and the heaps of rotted manure / pushed over frosty paths on still / midwinter days, or when an east wind / chewed at our knuckles" (*PT* 42). The garden planting was filled with strain and worry: "We built this garden together, husband; / germinated seeds in early spring, / gambling with a crystal dice, / moon calendars and almanacs, / risked seedlings to a late black frost, / wept at loss—but some survived / to thrive a summer of aching backs" (*PT* 43).

The rare appearance of the word *husband* in Meehan's poetic oeuvre coincides in this poem with a female narrator cast as a version of Eve, her former garden "ferociously passing judgement" (*PT* 42). The narrator's departure has effectively undomesticated the garden by allowing nature to make its own choices. Hence, while she finds "the peas holding for dear life to their sticks," alongside the "smaller drowning salad stuff," the weeds "grow lush and lovely / at midsummer, honeysuckle roving / through the hawthorn" (*PT* 42). In this poem human agency is subject to larger forces, and the narrator's alignment with "a song of fate, of fortune, of a journey" (*PT* 44) has carried her beyond the limits of the domestic enclosure.

Once again, Meehan presents the necessity of these limits being breached as the condition for confronting communal wounds. Rather than an escape into romantic love, the marriage is, for the narrator, a healing of relations with what turn out to be inseparable entities, her ancestors and the earth:

> I did not cast it off lightly,
> the yoke of work, the years of healing,
> of burying my troubled dead
> with every seed committed to the earth,
> judging their singular, particular needs,
> nurturing them with sweat and prayer
> to let the ghosts go finally from me
> with every basket of the harvest

> I garnered in golden light for our table,
> something singing in me all the while,
> a song of fate, of fortune, of a journey,
> a twisty road that led away from you,
> my husband of the sea-scarred eyes. (*PT* 44)

As in so many of Meehan's poems, the private experience in "Not alone . . ." is ultimately situated in a larger public context. Bourgeois insularity will not hold. The narrator has appeased her "troubled dead," healing her own haunting by ancestral trauma through an active relationship with the land. Yet, paradoxically, her labor in the garden has led her beyond its limits. Her healing is coupled with departure; the bounty of these years of work is the finding of another road. Thus, what seems to have been learned in the "garden" of bourgeois marriage is that rescue of the self through romantic love is a narrative that must be relinquished. There is no real escape into an insular domesticity or no lasting escape.

The point is elaborated in "A Different Eden," in which the mythological history and significance of the garden with its gendered implications is fully owned. The poem appears fourth in "Berlin Diary, 1991," a complex sequence of seven sections that refigures gender relations in the context of Germany's racial and ethnic history. In this way, the colonial dimension of the garden trope re-emerges in *Pillow Talk*. Once again, Meehan investigates the perilousness of resting entirely on romantic love, this time in the context of genocide and ethnic cleansing. Meehan reframes gender relations as one more case of relations with the Other. That is, romantic love emerges as an especially intense negotiation with difference—a negotiation in which the temptation is either to dominate and degrade the Other or reduce the Other to a version of the same.

An alternative relation with the Other appears in "A Different Eden," where the Christian garden story as a myth of origins is reread by restoring its occluded dimensions. This poem unmakes the garden story by unearthing the "suppressed genesis" of the first female inhabitant of Eden:

> The morning I left Dublin you were telling me a story—
> a suppressed genesis. How Lilith
> who pre-dated Eve went about the garden
> and asked each creature, each plant,
> to tell her its original name.
> I pictured her stooped to a mandrake. *Mandragora*
>   *Officianarum.*
> What the plant said to her,
> or she to it for that matter, is a mystery. (*PT* 49)

As a figure predating Eve, Lilith serves to relocate the origins of the garden and, indeed, to make of it a "different" place. Rather than Adamic colonizing of nature and domination through naming—"*You Giraffe! Me God's man!*"—Lilith seeks a dialogue with "each creature, each plant" (*PT* 49), establishing reciprocal relations with the land and the creatures that assume their difference and their agency. Thus, only nonhuman nature knows "its original name" and is able to tell it.

Note, too, that Lilith "asks" for the names: she recognizes the unique integrity of each responding life. Moreover, the image of the mandrake gestures toward Lilith's own status in the garden. In the medieval text by Ben Sira, Lilith appears as the unruly first wife of Adam who asserts her equality: "Both of us are equal because both of us are from the earth." Because Adam insists on her subordination, Lilith leaves the garden in protest, and Adam is given a more compliant mate (Vogelsang 150). But in Meehan's "A Different Eden," Lilith models the relations with the Other she might have expected from Adam. Indeed, Meehan's poem suggests that Lilith's anti-hierarchism finds its source, as in the Ben Sira text, in common earthly origins. And by singling out the mandrake, the narrator's imaginative extension of a story that begins in Dublin casts a self-fertile plant as the focus of Lilith's attention (the mandrake's flowers are hermaphroditic, just as Lilith herself represents a self-sustaining autonomy). In this way, the poem is dialogues all the way down—between the "you" of the poem and the narrator, between the narrator and the genesis story, between Lilith and the mandrake, and, finally, between the mandrake and itself. Thus, in this poem Meehan relaunches the female subject from a different garden.

Having shed the illusion of rescue through the garden of romantic love, Meehan's narrators perform the work of self-rescue. In doing so, they are made strong enough to step into a powerful communal role of advocate and witness for all. In the poems that immediately follow "A Different Eden," the figure of nested Russian dolls appears and reappears. In these poems, the smallest, inmost doll of birch heartwood serves as an emblem of the inner child who must be rescued, healed, and protected. The incantation that closes the sequence "The Wounded Child"—"Rescue the child / from her dark spell! / Rescue the child / from her dark spell! / Rescue the child" (*PT* 59)—is immediately followed by "She-Who-Walks-Among-the-People," in which the narrator rejects the old scripts of female victimization and defeat, and instead asks her granny for another story: "Tell me the story about the kind lady / who became a great warrior in the old days" (*PT* 60). In the request itself, the phrases "kind lady" and "great warrior" assume the compatibility of compassionate civility and fierce combative strength in the body of a woman. Perhaps recalling the status of women in preconquest Ireland, this alternative narrative represents a reclaimed female agency in the service of community broadly defined. Indeed, this woman warrior addresses "a bad spell" "cast on the whole island": "The people lived / in fear and pain. The land itself was hurting, / as were the animals who shared it with the people" (*PT* 60). That a reintegrated and reconstituted female subject speaks and acts in the service of the whole—the people, the land, and the animals—suggests Meehan's vision of healing interconnection.

In these poems recasting the female subject, Meehan avoids any simple reversal of gender politics that might position women, rather than men, at the top of a social hierarchy. Nor has she figured women as essentially closer to nature and therefore responsible for the interrelations of humans and nature, or what ecofeminist philosopher Val Plumwood has described as replacing "'the angel in the house' with 'the angel in the ecosystem'" (*Mastery of Nature* 9). Rather, poems like "My Father Perceived as a Vision of St. Francis"—the opening poem of *Pillow Talk*—demonstrate that Meehan's transformed garden relations involve restoring the full range of human capacities to both women and men. Such a change allows for a broadly human partnership and reciprocity with nonhuman nature. In "My Father . . . ," the garden's permeable boundaries (neither entrapping nor excluding) allow the "dawn whinny" of a piebald horse next door to wake the narrator to her father's domestic stirrings: "I heard / him rake the ash from the grate, / plug in the kettle, hum a snatch of a tune" (*PT* 11). This paternal ease at the hearth opens to a nurturing exchange with nature outdoors. The narrator watches her father greet the dawn with what is apparently a daily ritual, the feeding of birds from near and far, a connection with the gift of flight that renders constructed human boundaries superfluous. In the "vision" of the title of the poem, the father moves past any stereotype of the dominating patriarch, for he is "older than I had reckoned, / his hair completely silver / and for the first time I saw the stoop / of his shoulder, saw that / his leg was stiff " (*PT* 11). The narrator's perception of her father's protean, aging body gives rise to a re-visioning of the male presence in the garden through an alternative Christian saint:

> The garden was a pandemonium
> when my father threw up his hands
> and tossed the crumbs to the air. The sun
>
> cleared O'Reilly's chimney
> and he was suddenly radiant,
> a perfect vision of St. Francis,
> made whole, made young again,
> in a Finglas garden. (*PT* 12)

Androcentric mastery has given way to human humility; the father freely gives up control to a commotion of bread and wings moving in air. The scene might remind us of one of ecocriticism's founding texts, Lynn White Jr.'s "The Historical Roots of Our Ecological Crisis," in which St. Francis emerges as "a patron saint for ecologists." White argues that the "greatest spiritual revolutionary in Western history, Saint Francis, proposed what he thought was an alternative Christian view of nature and man's relation to it: he tried to substitute the idea of the equality of all creatures, including man, for the idea of man's limitless rule of creation" (14). In Meehan's new garden, Adam has finally learned Lilith's lesson of reciprocal relations. His nourishing gesture restores him to youth, "radiant" and "whole."

After *Pillow Talk*, only a few echoes of the old trope of the garden sound in Meehan's collections. The working through and transforming of the figure and all it represents has been largely achieved. Indeed, in *Dharmakaya* (2000), it is as if the poet has become the "kind lady" and "great warrior" conjured in "She-Who-Walks-Among-the-People." These poems of communal witness address the continuing class trauma of Dublin's inner city in the wake of Ireland's colonization by global capitalism. In *Dharmakaya*, the act of remaking the colonial and bourgeois dimensions of the garden appears explicitly in "Literacy Class, Southern Inner City," in which both the narrator and her adult female students work to live and write beyond the traumas of a church schooling that has left multiple wounds: "Without tricks, // without wiles, with no time to waste now, we plant / words on these blank fields. It is an unmapped world / and we are pioneering agronomists launched onto this strange planet, / the sad flag of the home place newly furled" (*D* 51). In this poem, the land is returned to its role as source of life and nourishment. By appearing not as enclosure but as open field, the land is figuratively reclaimed by those dispossessed through the internal colonizations of gender and class enforced by the church. Witnessing to class trauma takes the narrator and her students into "an unmapped world" where they seek to pioneer an art of self-restoration that does not rely on domination. Indeed, the image of the unfurled flag of conquest appears here as the "newly furled" flag of divestment, agronomy practiced in a new key.

The work of self-reclamation in the garden poems is not separate from this kind of communal vision but rather an integral part of it. Meehan has said, "I think I have always had that strong sense of landscape, community, and selfhood as the triangulation for the work" (Allen Randolph, "Body Politic" 264). The project of dismantling the garden as emblem of empire, bourgeois privilege, and oppressive gender relations makes way in *Dharmakaya* for the recovery of the garden as the site of healing and reciprocal relations with the earth. In "Recovery," Meehan moves beyond the characteristic opposition between wild and domesticated, finding an appropriately middle way in this Buddhist-informed volume: the gardener "is sweeping / the moss garden free / of fallen husks of moss blossom / and other debris" (*D* 60). Harmony and balance between human and nonhuman nature emerge in this first stanza with the sweeping arc of image and line—short lines alternating with longer, the upright letters of *bl* surrounded by *moss* in "moss blossom," the sound sense of "free" and "debris." This garden is freed by a human agency, working "gently" on an appropriate scale, and in an attitude of reverence. The gardener has not only "bowed to the ground" she tends, but she has also gone "down on her knees there."

An echo of Lilith "stooped to a mandrake" links this recovered garden to its counterpart in "A Different Eden." But in "Recovery," no misguided Adam is named. Machines appear as overwrought human tools destructive of an animate nature. There is no subtlety or care in their "trail blazing," which has been their relentless work since "dawn" (*D* 60). Those behind their "whine" go unnamed—one way of suggesting, perhaps, that a masculinist manner with its purely instrumental use of nature may be picked up or discarded by either sex. Moreover, Meehan seems here to evoke state-sanctioned multinationals at work: removed, faceless, and so invisible that the narrator "cannot see them." As the poem turns abruptly back to its immediate setting, an anthropocentric relation to nature is dismissed and rendered a fallen world that exists outside the garden the narrator has reclaimed by emulating the Eastern art of caretaking. As if to signal a relationship with the land that is mutual, the language closing the poem moves toward intersubjectivity: homeplace and garden merge in the ambiguity of "sweep clear a bed," the tending of garden and narrator inseparable. As in Meehan's beloved medieval poem "The Hermit's Hut," "Recovery" gives us a narrator who is fully resident in nature, her "mossy pillow" neither entirely human artifact nor untouched flora. Through recovery of a garden where, in Carolyn Merchant's words, "the practice of gardening is a caretaking of the soil and the life it generates," Meehan's narrator also aspires to recover herself and her own health (*Reinventing Eden* 26).

The wry, postmodern Eden of "Deadwood," in Meehan's collection *Painting Rain* (2009), is the garden poem we might have expected after following the trope through the earlier books. The opening line populates the garden with equal partners, signaled by the grammatically balanced caesura of "Me with the secateurs, you with the Greek saw." Matched in power, the "me" and "you" come together in "we," like adept dancers who are capable of moving as one: "we cut the creeper back, we prune the rose" (*PR* 17). The mutual project of this pair is precisely to reclaim the garden by clearing away the dead limbs and, we come to understand, the dead narratives that block new growth. A recast love poem, this technically playful sonnet is arranged in three airy quatrains, the stanza breaks letting in light and space as if after pruning. Here the male partner is the punning image of the phallocentric: "Your tool's honed edge // whines as it goes. All day you lay down the law" (*PR* 17). And the playful undercutting is even-handed: "god knows / I'm as bad with my cranks and my post op / critique of your handiwork" (*PR* 17). An unconventional rhyme scheme, *abcd* repeated until the final couplet, allows for the inventive diminishing rhyme of "chop," "lop," and "op," a snip, snip, snip across stanzas until the

final coupling of "floor" and "lore" lands with a mutual send-up.
The ease, whimsy, and self-awareness of the voice in "Deadwood"
is a triumph of craft and perspective. We can gauge it fully when we
consider it alongside the garden snapshot in "The Pattern" in *The
Man Who Was Marked by Winter*, which is the Meehan poem that
most explicitly addresses mother-and-daughter relations:

> There's a photo of her taken in Phoenix Park
> alone on a bench surrounded by roses
> as if she had been born to formal gardens.
> She stares out as if unaware
> that any human hand held the camera, wrapped
> entirely in her own shadow, the world beyond her
> already a dream, already lost. She's
> eight months pregnant. Her last child. (*MMW* 19)

Captured unaware in an old seat of empire, the mother in "The
Pattern" offers no reliable guidance for negotiating colonial,
class, or gender scripts. Only her negative example informs. She is
"unaware / that any hand held the camera," and she is also unconscious that she is framed by her culture's social constructions—an
omission of education and experience the narrator suggests in the
rest of the poem she is determined to rectify in her own life. For
the mother is "wrapped / entirely in her own shadow," a Jungian
allusion to unwitting self-victimization. We see this again in the
unconscious figure of the mother after a suicide attempt in "This
Is Not a Confessional Poem" in *Painting Rain*. Both poetic episodes
are set in gardens, in which the historical accretions of that built
environment come devastatingly to bear. Indeed, Phoenix Park,
with its resonances of nineteenth-century Anglo-Irish colonial
horticulture (as well as of assassination of colonial officials) is an
apt context for a mother and daughter living out the consequences
of multiple oppressions. To work on this contested ground, carefully
transforming the old tropes, is the large and ongoing of project of
Paula Meehan's work.

INTERVIEW

··

RELISHING THE CONVERSATION, 2020

KATHRYN KIRKPATRICK: One of the things about "Six Sycamores" that I love is the ways that you make the natural world so animate, the various parts of the house so wanting to go back to where they came from. And then I just love your craft in the sonnets! In number 51 you've got *wild* and *exiled* rhyming and then *desire* and *fire*. Yes! You know, it's like that sonnet where you've got the diminishing rhyme . . ."Deadwood"! I discovered that, and I was so happy. And I thought, "Okay, that's why I'm writing about these poems!"

PAULA MEEHAN: I've always loved you as a reader, because most people don't even notice such things! I know many times in my life when I'd say about a poet, "Wow! Look at what they're doing. Oh, they're so performative, showing off." And it's lovely. I mean that's something that I really love in the different traditions. One of the big conversations I had with Eavan Boland was about where your craft is in danger of becoming just an ornamentation. You can lose sight of the energy that moves the poem or even sometimes, in a worst-case scenario, you could lose sight of your truth. And part of me loves to balance along that edge. The part of me that welcomes art for art's sake, money for God's sake, is also part of it. I have no problem with art for art's sake; the more of it, the better.

I also believe that the things worth doing are worth doing for nothing. There are all the struggles as a worker, and I believe a poet is someone who deserves to be paid and we should know our worth as artists. But beyond that, there is also a moment when your community may not have money to support a poem. So, there is that moment where the drive to make has to make a jump, and that's why poetry is such a sacred tradition too, because it's probably the least easily monetized. It's a kind of a calling that is determined by more than the need for a wage.

I really embrace the patterning impulse in poetry; I understand that the pattern of the life may also be part of the mix. Some patterns have a very long repeat, especially cross-generational, but the patterning is so much part of the mnemonic. And it's through repetition and variation of the repeat that we begin to understand the world and that we evolve and that we survive.

If I'm moderating workshops, I always emphasize the importance of finding, learning, and understanding patterns. Anyone who has heard a lot of songs or learned a lot of songs has a fantastic quiver full of arrows—a hoard of lines to draw out from the song tradition. In our traditions patterning is central. If you go back to the folk roots of all, or most, of the received forms, then I think you can rediscover their original energy. If you remember that the villanelle was probably a slave song, that the sonnet was an agricultural song about the different ways animals take each other, "little song" of Sicily in the thirteenth century—the boar taking the sow, the rooster the hen, the bull the heifer—if you remember the ballad was a song, the ode a dance: you feel that the form has its roots in clay, the foul rag-and-bone shop of the heart.

KK: I love that you make those connections, and it's interesting that you brought up Eavan Boland. I was going to ask you about the conversations you would have had with her.

PM: Yes.

KK: That in itself could be an essay. "The Conversations I Would Have Had with Eavan Boland" would be a beautiful piece. I'm wondering about that loss, the role she played in your life and work.

PM: Eavan was the outside assessor of my master's thesis at Eastern Washington University.

KK: I don't think I knew that!

PM: I taught English 101 every morning at an obscene hour for a
night owl like myself—7:30 or 8:30—every single morning
for two years I spent in Washington State. Each semester I
taught English 101, Writing American English, but I didn't
even speak American English! I was straight from Dublin
where English is delighted in, abused, murdered, a sonic wilderness to the uninitiated. And I would have indulged in my
own narrow little square mile of Dublin Northside Inner
City English, which is not even Hiberno English. I thought
it was very funny that I was there as a teacher of a language
I didn't even speak, and it was the students themselves, a different cohort every few months, who taught me American
English. Every single first-year undergraduate in the university had to pass the exam at the end of the course—whatever
their calling, from ballet dancer to scientist. The wrestlers
and the footballers, the athletic scholarship students, were
the funniest ones because I'd have their coaches on my case,
coming in to see me, talking about "my boys" or "my girls"
and the importance of getting them through that darned
exam. I remember one wrestler who was just gorgeous. A
lovely man. He had wonderful stories about South Side
Chicago, where he grew up. He wrote phonetically about his
people, and I loved it. But I had to get him through the re-
quirements of the English Department's 101 exam at the end
because you only had them for that one term, and they had
to be able to write a three-point essay with an introduction.
And they had to know how to do at least a basic amount of
research to get through the university. I had these amazing
students. They taught me so much. They really opened up
their lives to me. Once a week, I would use a poem, a short
poem: could be from anywhere. It could be like a prayer or a
little bit of Gary Snyder. Could be an Irish poem and translation. Just a little, maybe a few small lines, and we did a bit
of free writing while images came. And I would use Eavan's
poems regularly—there were often young mothers in the class.

KK: Yes.

PM: And they would see themselves reflected in the poetry. I would try and get the measure of them. I think each of the classes was about thirty [students], so I couldn't give a great deal of individual attention, but the things I found out in these sessions! Jim McAuley, my teacher, thesis advisor, and director of the creative writing program at Eastern, the Dublin man and poet, knew that I was doing this. Secretly, unbeknownst to me but to please me, to surprise me, he enlisted Eavan as my outside examiner. I couldn't believe it. I was so humbled and thrilled. And the letter she wrote about my thesis, which was essentially the manuscript for what became my first book, it was a one-page response she wrote, and it was on one of those old typewriters where the typeface is different degrees of darkness and indentation, and I think the "e" was a little bit crooked. A clear simple letter warning against becoming picturesque, and also in a deeper sense not to become a martyr to my gift. The way, say, Brendan Behan became a martyr to drink, you know. And John McGahern gave me very similar advice when I was in his workshop—to refuse the allure of being lionized. And Eavan was just brilliantly incisive about what I was doing. When I started teaching back in Dublin and was running workshops with Jim, the EWU summer programs, I would invite her to visit those workshops. And she would come in, and so I would see her in action with the students, and I learned a huge amount from her that way. And that was about 1983 or '4, and that's when our conversations and our arguments really intensified. She was a central and necessary part of my journey.

There have been other losses. The reality is that as my friends die, as my teachers die, the conversation ends but only in the mortal realm. I still talk to them and listen for a reply. I think of the conversations I would have had with Ciaran Carson, long rambling excursions in the etymological highroads and byways. I look at a word and say, "Ah, Ciaran would love that," because that was his whole thing, the dictionary angel—chasing the word. Find the root, find where the word comes from, which language? How did it come into English? Why is it absolutely right for this moment in this poem? And those kind of conversations I can have with Theo as well because he's close to me, shares this preoccupation. You relish the times you've had the conversation and the argument because it was a time also of hilarity and companionship, often on tour, walking the cities, at the galleries and museums, intense, involved, at festivals often with music, celebrating ourselves and the world.

5

BEYOND HUMAN
EXCEPTIONALISM

———

In her tenure as Ireland Professor of Poetry, Paula Meehan made human relations with the more-than-human world central to her lectures, first in Belfast in November 2013 with "Imaginary Bonnets with Real Bees in Them," then in Dublin in November 2014 with "The Solace of Artemis," and finally in Belfast in 2015 with "Planet Water." This chapter explores the ways Meehan continues the critical ecofeminist and ecopolitical project of her poetry in these innovative, shape-shifting lectures, where a speaker ever aware of the ways our representations of nonhuman animals produce consequences for actual humans and animals alike takes her formal and conceptual cues from the dances of bees and the mitochondrial DNA of bears.

Moving beyond the binaries of poetry and prose, art and science, intuition and logic, literature and politics, among others, Meehan offers powerful correctives to the Cartesian dualisms that stymie our relations with the more-than-human world. As such, these lectures move us beyond the limits of the discourse of human exceptionalism by offering a human voice in dialogue with the bears and the bees.

INTERSPECIES DEPENDENCIES

The project of many posthumanist, ecofeminist, and animal studies scholars—there are many intersections among these perspectives—is precisely, as Paul Waldau put it in his *Animal Studies, An Introduction*, to demystify and unseat a tradition of human exceptionalism, "an exclusivist, human-centered agenda" that "dominates, reshapes, and destroys so many domains in our more-than-human world" (159). Val Plumwood has identified human exceptionalism as "the hyperseparation of humans as a special species and the reduction of non-humans to their usefulness to humans" ("Active Voice" 35–36). For Plumwood, the perspective is inimical to humans and nonhumans alike: "it distorts our perceptions and enframings in ways that make us insensitive to limits, dependencies and interconnections of a non-human kind" ("Active Voice" 36). Plumwood and, later, Donna Haraway, find that a human exceptionalist view fails to acknowledge Darwin's central insight about the continuity of all life and the kinship of humans with other life forms: as "a spatial and temporal web of interspecies dependencies," *Homo sapiens* is "firmly in the world of other critters all trying to make an earthly living and so evolving in relation to one another without the sureties of directional signposts that culminate in Man" (Haraway 11). This dismantling of humans as fixed and separate arbiters of a living, multispecies planet is, as I have been arguing, part of Meehan's poetic project as well.

An emphasis on dialogue within an animate multispecies planet spans the decades of Meehan's work. As in her early poem "One Evening in May," Meehan's first Poetry Professor lecture locates the vocation of poet and the process of writing poetry within an organismic worldview where nature is full of agency. In this poem from her 1994 collection, *Pillow Talk*, an animate nonhuman world actively instructs the narrator with a vision of the archaic Earth Mother, origin and destination of all life. The unbidden encounter enraptures the speaker with a glimpse of cosmic otherness, the Earth Mother appearing as a composite of the many-breasted and snake goddesses, nurturing source and skin-shedding transformer. In a striking ecofeminist poetic gesture, the narrator is mastered by and put at the service of a shape-shifting Earth Mother, not only "alive, sensitive, and responsive to human actions," but with quite definite plans of her own:

> It's just her style to trick about
>
> shapechanging all the while.
> Whatever happens now, I'll be bound
> to her rule for life. I pray I'll not rue
> the day she parted clouds,
>
> revealed her starry body, her great
> snakeshead, her myriad children
> feasting at her breasts. She spoke. She said,
> 'You're mine. Come. Do my bidding.' (*PT* 16)

Two decades later, as Poetry Professor of Ireland, Meehan opens her first public lecture with a strikingly similar description of the poetic process:

> Poetry can usefully be considered as a negotiation in words be-
> tween no-mind and mind, between that place where attention
> is at rest in the void, open to inspiration from otherwhere, and
> that human place in conscious, directed attention where the
> rigour of craft finds its natural home. Here, then, are nine short
> meditations on poetry—on the obsessive, on craft and inspira-
> tion, on the apparently wayward but always mysteriously pur-
> poseful flight of bees in my bonnet. (*Imaginary Bonnets* 3)

Having passed through the transformative, Buddhist-inflected poems of her fifth collection, *Dharmakaya*, Meehan now employs another language—no-mind, otherwhere, and the void—to de-scribe what has here become a seasoned partnership, a negotiation, between the human and the nonhuman forces of nature. And this exchange is figured as "the mysteriously purposeful flight of bees," nonhuman creatures with the unsettling capacity to sting, buzzing about their own business in a woman poet's headgear. Beyond the binary of "imaginary" and "real," actual bees in the poet's garden at once come for the borage and become the poet's "undersong," suggestively inspiring the structure of a lecture that proceeds not through a strict, linear logic but more like the bees' communicative dance, through "intricate signals with coded information" (*Imaginary Bonnets* 4). The lectures, then, are neither poetry nor prose, but something in between, "meditations" where the associative meets the narrative and motifs are given new contexts, and then transformed and reintroduced in another shape.

READING ANIMALS: THE BEES

In "Imaginary Bonnets with Real Bees in Them," Meehan does not acquiesce to the colloquial meaning of "You have a bee in your bonnet," where the nonhuman animal is figured as a nuisance and the bonnet-wearer as unreasonably obsessed by what others do not find important, pest and pesterer alike annoying in the human world. Rather, she reclaims the idiom and allies herself with the bees. The gesture unfolds dramatically at a decisive moment in her life as a Catholic schoolgirl when conflicts with the nuns come to a head over grief for her newly dead dog, Prince, whom she eulogizes in a poem rather than completing an assigned composition on milk: "I wrote an elegy. I didn't have that word then. *Elegy*. Poor dog. Poor dead dog. Miss Shannon thought I was up to something" (3). For love of another animal, the young Meehan pushes back at the supposed infraction. Threatened with expulsion, she faces the charge from Sister Philippa of having "a bee in my bonnet," and astonishes herself by replying "'Better bees in my bonnet than bats in the belfry'" (9). Although the young Meehan seems to exchange one animal insult for another, we might read the "better" as her embrace of the intimate human-animal relation established with bees rather than any denigration of bats. Indeed, the lecture's next section takes up the seventh-century "body of Brehon Law in relation to bees," where both humans and animals have protections: "The laws remind us we had ancestors who knew the need to articulate, to be precise in language, in order to be fair to the bees and to the humans who had the need of them" (*Imaginary Bonnets* 10). As so often in Meehan's work, this meditation on bees looks to the past in order to imagine a future. Describing the immunity Brehon law gave to bees if they should attack, Meehan recounts that "[a]mong the complete immunities in bee-judgments according to Irish law is the man on whom they have rushed when robbing them, moving them, seizing them [or] looking at them over their hives at the time they are swarming" (*Imaginary Bonnets* 11). Meehan sets this bio-centric vision side by side with our current treatment of bees as commodified objects, pointedly calling to account the then Minister for Agriculture of Ireland who failed to vote for an European Union two-year moratorium on the use of neonicotinoid pesticides, which harm bees and, by extension, the human community that depends on them.

"Imaginary Bonnets with Real Bees in Them" interweaves the language of bees with any number of human activities and thereby works at the linguistic level to blur the boundaries between human and nonhuman animals. The "world wide web" becomes "a kind of hive mind," where Meehan finds an image of the ancient Myanmar bee, making a "beeline" to the dictionary where the Greek word for honey, *meli*, leads her to "feeling fiercely mel-livorous" and then to her last tin of Ikarian honey, brought back from the island of Ikaria. Thus, seeking to rejoin the sign with its signifier, Meehan traces the etymologies of words back to their connections with the material world:

> The individual words have autonomous force, I would say magic power, in terms of their auditory force on the physical body, and the shadow power too in the ghost life of the word, the etymol-ogy, the discreet history that each word carries with it, etymolo-gies that if we could trace far enough back might be analogous to hearing the buzzing of the one hundred million-year-old bee in amber. (*Imaginary Bonnets* 19)

This evocation of the incantatory power of language gestures, as we will see in chapter 6, toward the poems of *Geomantic* (2016), which Meehan was writing during her tenure as Poetry Professor of Ireland.

BETWEEN SCIENCE AND ART

In *Critical Ecofeminism* Greta Gaard retrieves Plumwood's insight that the human exceptionalism prevalent in the dominant culture of Western societies extends to many scientists themselves. For Plumwood and for Gaard, Darwin's central insights "remain only superficially absorbed" because "the traditional scientific project of technological control is justified by continuing to think of humans as a special superior species set apart and entitled to manipulate and commodify the earth for their own benefit" (Gaard 45–46). Meehan's second Poetry Professor of Ireland lecture, "The Solace of Artemis," realigns relations between science and art. Written for Iggy McGovern's *20/12: Twenty Irish Poets Respond to Science in Twelve Lines*, the poem on which the lecture is based models for its initial audience, delegates to the European Science Open Forum in 2012, an undoing of the human/animal binary by using scientific data to recast myth. Meehan employs the trope of shape-shifting, in this case between narrator and bear, to re-vision human and nonhuman animal futures, in the process subverting distorted cultural dualisms between science and art. By examining Meehan's lecture and poem, I explore the ways her postmodern representations of nonhuman animals involve a rethinking of human *as* animal in what Steve Baker has described as "a wholly serious creative attempt 'to imagine differently reconstituted communities and selves' and to heal the destructively fragmented experience of the contemporary world" (25). Meehan's postmodern, posthuman vision engages with a premodern sensibility to restore the critical interdependence between human and nonhuman animals, which modern cultures have sought to erase.

READING ANIMALS: BEARS

The iconic face of climate change, polar bears are often shown clinging to nubs of melting ice. We hear reports of cubs who drown because they cannot make it across vast expanses of water. We learn that adults have taken to eating each other in a desperate search for food. Sea ice has declined "at a linear rate of 14% per decade from 1979 through 2011" (IUCN Red List) and with it the energy-saving "sit and wait" hunting beside ice holes of the polar bear, whose reliance on the fat of seals cannot be made up with land-based foods. With the vanishing of the icy environment to which they are adapted, these apex predators of the Arctic are using four times as much energy, often through extended fasting, to survive. Without a significant course correction in carbon dioxide emissions, starvation awaits most polar bears, and most of their populations are likely to be gone by 2100, the remaining clusters surviving only in the planet's last location for year-round ice, "the Queen Elizabeth Islands—the northernmost cluster in Canada's Arctic archipelago" (Dickie). Indeed, because of the melting of Arctic ice at the North Pole, polar bear populations, in what is called a "directional gene flow," are now slowly converging on what may be their final refuge in this icy Canadian archipelago, these ninety-four islands north of mainland Canada most likely to have year-round sea ice (Fears).

Through a subtle and evocative image of what climate change means for the bears themselves, Subhankar Banerje photographed bear dens in 2002, warning viewers that the sole conservation area for denning polar bears in the United States, the Arctic National Wildlife Refuge Coastal Plain, is threatened by ongoing pressure from companies like Shell for access to oil and gas. In contrast to Banerje's biocentric perspective, the April 2008 cover of *Time* magazine made use of an increasingly well-established visual discourse in which polar bears at once signify catastrophic climate change and become part of its collateral damage. The *Time* cover of a lone polar bear on a fragment of ice was unapologetically anthropocentric; the fate of the polar bears, the cover suggested, is sealed. They are now of interest only as an indicator of how climate change "affects you, your kids and their kids as well." The heavy representational freight polar bears have now assumed locks them firmly into a narrative of catastrophe. By wresting her polar bear out of that narrative, Meehan suggests that one strategy human beings might take in the face of climate crisis is to imagine and live into a world where human beings partner with nature's resilience:

The Solace of Artemis

I read that every polar bear alive has mitochondrial DNA
from a common mother, an Irish brown bear who once
roved out across the last ice age, and I am comforted.
It has been a long hot morning with the children of the
    machine,

their talk of memory, of buying it, of buying it cheap, but I,
memory keeper by trade, scan time coded in the golden hive
    mind
of eternity. I burn my books, I burn my whole archive:
a blaze that sears, synapses flaring cell to cell where

memory sleeps in the wax hexagonals of my doomed and
    melting comb.
I see him loping towards me across the vast ice field
to where I wait in the cave mouth, dreaming my cubs about
    the den,
my honied ones, smelling of snow and sweet oblivion.
(*Imaginary Bonnets* 30)

A U.S. Geological Survey study confirms that today's polar bears "stem from one or several hybridization events with brown bears" (Fears), and, indeed, mitochondrial DNA from now-extinct Irish brown bears reveals they are clear ancestors for at least some polar bear populations (Press Association). Moreover, the imaginative citizen science of Meehan's poem continues to hold—a new hybrid dubbed the "pizzly" or "grolar bear" has appeared in the Canadian Arctic. With a first sighting in 2006, this hybrid of the genetically similar brown bear and polar bear is fully fertile and represents adaptations not only in polar bears forced on land because of less Arctic ice but also grizzlies hibernating for shorter periods who range into polar bear territories (Jex). This possible future for survival is the terrain Meehan's poem takes up. In doing so, "The Solace of Artemis" engages with what David Farrier has described as our Anthropocene experience of living with the convergence of deep geological and evolutionary time in the present. In these terms, poetry can provide us with "a point of confluence between deep pasts and deep futures" (Farrier 19) where environmental background becomes foreground, and familiarity with deep time is recovered in the uncanny temporalities of the "'uneven and mul-tivalent' present" (Farrier 19). Meehan's poem imagines a deep future by retrieving the deep past.

The poem performs the process of this reimagining of the future by recounting, for an audience of scientists (who have been notably stymied by their inability to rouse the world's human cit-izens and governments to meaningful action in the face of climate change), the role that an art and literature engaged in the making of new cultural myths from scientific data might play in changing public consciousness. Indeed, reinforcing the cultural work the poem performs, Meehan chose as the topic of her second Poetry Professor of Ireland lecture, given at Trinity College Dublin, an unpacking of this very poem for yet another public audience. In a lecture by the same title, "The Solace of Artemis," she empha-sized the important role of scientific data in the poem's making by naming as her inspiration published research in the journal *Current Biology* conducted by teams of scientists at Trinity, Penn State, and Oxford. Thus, in her poem Meehan performs for her initial scientific audience a speaker in the act of recasting the story of the polar bear as poetry, using the findings of other scientists and in the process evoking the convergence of deep geological and evolutionary time in the present. Later, she performs the poem again, on this occasion with the initial scientific audience in the frame, so that the Trinity lecture also becomes a modeling of how a poet might educate and be educated by scientists as new cultural myths for the Anthropocene are collaboratively made.

"I read," "The Solace of Artemis" opens, asserting that the act of taking in new information from the scientific community will be the making of this poem and the new myth it constructs. That nineteen-syllable opening line, beyond, as poet Mary Oliver observes, "the pentameter line [which] most nearly matches the breath capacity of our English lungs" (40), immediately takes us beyond the ordinary, into what Oliver describes as the "greater-than-human" implications of the long poetic line: "It can seem by its simple endurance—beyond ordinary lung capacity—grandiose, prophetic. It can also indicate abundance, richness, a sense of joy" as well as forces "unstoppable" (41). We might also say we're taken by such long lines into the cyclical *kyros* time of myth. In this opening line, the perfect iambic pentameter of "I read that every polar bear alive" finds its mate, its almost match, in the nine syllables that follow, where the iambic lope ends in other pairings, the double spondee of "—al DNA." Heavily packed with the scientific data that has seeded the poem, the grammatical sentence moves across three poetic lines, two of them enjambed, with a movement if not sprightly, then certainly unstoppable.

Meehan thus has us perform the act of reading and the taking in of new scientific information with her narrator. And then the narrator models for us not the familiar discourse of catastrophe, or, rather, not human passivity in the face of climate catastrophe—for the poem embodies a deep awareness of our perilous condition—but instead how we might respond imaginatively, critically, even now. The poem works its meanings as strong poems do, through craft. The diffuse *m*, *n*, and *r* sounds of the second line evoke the genetic boundary-blurring the poem names as do the echoes of *common* in the words that flank it, fro*m* and *m*other, a linguistic echoing of genetic echoes. Unfolding in the present tense, "I read," "I am," those first three lines carry us into the process of the poem's making, performing for us the possibility of comfort rather than despair. In the long view, the polar bears themselves are the result of an adaptation and a strategy for survival. A wily intelligence is at work in the world, a resourcefulness and a resilience. Should we see fit as a species to cease what we know to be destructive, we might thereby find some hope, something on which to rely. At the very least, it has given this speaker comfort and solace. As Meehan herself described her response to the scientists' findings about polar bears:

> In the face of anxiety about our future and that of the many creatures with whom we share this amazing creation, their research offered the comfort of the longer view, the prospect that though we live in cataclysmic times, something will survive. Can we live with the idea, though, that it may not be us? (*Imaginary Bonnets* 29)

As the lecture, "The Solace of Artemis" reverberates with the poem, we might read the "us" who may not survive most obviously as the human species and its own coming extinction. Or we might, along with the shape-shifting narrator of Meehan's last stanza, consider that another way of being human might allow for animal survival, human and nonhuman alike. It would be a posthuman that is not "us" but rather an adaptive version of us. The shape-shifting gesture is made in Meehan's lecture as well, where she invokes "the ancient Greek goddess Artemis, the bear mother, in whose protection I place myself, whose solace I profit from, in whose territory I build my den against the coming storm" (*Imaginary Bonnets* 30). Elsewhere in the lecture, mothers become mother bears, fathers father bears, the home a cave, this language a way of evoking "an older, wilder relationship with an animal self that might be truly at home in creation, free of dualism"

(*Imaginary Bonnets* 39). In these ways, then, Meehan might be said to be integrating scientific evidence into a larger project of healing the Cartesian dualism the Scientific Revolution itself helped to create. The narrator of her poem and the self she performs at her public lecture shape-shift between human and bear, neither human nor animal, but both.

MYTHS ARE TRUE

Meehan told her audience at Trinity in 2014 that her study of classical civilization as an undergraduate with the great classicist W. B. Stanford taught her that "myths are true":

> He would bring in examples from newspapers of the misuse of the word "myth"; it really annoyed him to see it misused as a homonym for lie, for untruth, for shaggy dog stories, for false science. "Myth," he would say, shaking the paper, "is the truth, the whole truth, and nothing but the truth." For the first time I began to see myth as the ancient truths of the ancestors, their poetry. (*Imaginary Bonnets* 32)

Meehan makes the connections throughout the lecture between myth, ritual, and poetry: for her, poems construct cultural myths that can give us guides for navigating difficult terrain, and the performance of the poem for audiences can serve as a ritual that has the potential to transform those who enter fully into the experience. While clearly well aware of the Auden-inflected debate about the limits of poetry for making things happen, Meehan's backward vision is long and her insistence on the communal role of the poet unflinching. Indeed, like her early mentor, Gary Snyder, she sees the poet's role as shamanic, including all the mystery, potential for healing, and responsibility to the tribe that word suggests. In the language of performance theory, her poems present opportunities for the culture to reflect upon itself, entertain alternatives to the status quo, and transform consciousness. In this sense, Meehan's "The

Solace of Artemis" embodies the possibility of allying the wisdom traditions of ancient myth with scientific discoveries to create new cultural building blocks.

MYTHOS AND *TECHNOS*

Meehan observes that her tandem reading as an undergraduate of classics, poetry, and science fiction inform her poetic vision:

> One of the commonest tropes in the science fiction I was reading was a group of humans landing on a far planet where all life, or sapient life at least, is extinct. They find a cave or a man-made bunker underground, a machine that holds the memory of some vanished human or human-related species, once top of the food chain, now perished due to misuse of resources, unquestioned indulgence of greed. They had failed as I fear we are failing to marry the resource and wisdom of *mythos* with the vaulting ambition and powers of *technos*. (*Imaginary Bonnets* 48)

If we return to Meehan's poem, we can see that it is precisely the possibility of wedding *mythos* and *technos* that offers comfort in the face of a mechanistic society given over to the latter. Maintaining its greater-than-human line lengths, "The Solace of Artemis" poem supplies the context in which the speaker particularly needed comfort; she has been among the children that a mechanistic capitalistic culture has created. These "children of the machine" have internalized the values of a world where everything is commodified, not least memory. The repetition in close proximity of "buying it" and "buying it cheap" evokes the capitalist accumulation mechanism of buying cheap and selling dear even as the clipped impatience of the abrupt plosive *t*'s, *b*'s, and *p* interrupt the pattern of diffuse, elongated sounds the poem has established. But in the face of the flash drive, the hard drive, and the cloud, this narrator offers the ancient resource of human memory and names the poet "memory keeper by trade." Reappropriating the language of the machine—"scan" and "coded"—for an organismic worldview, Meehan melds it with the nonhuman animal imagery of bees, "the golden hive mind" that features so prominently in "Imaginary Bonnets with Real Bees in Them." Appearing in this first lecture as the buzzing, wide-flung, communicative activity of the internet community, the hive of the second lecture goes up in flames, as Google itself admits it so easily could. Full of sizzling z's, s's, and soft c's, "blaze that sears, synapses flaring cell to cell where // memory sleeps," this second stanza burns down modern human historical time and along with it the culture of human exceptionalism that the field of critical animal studies describes as a doomed if illuminating dead end. Meehan finds it "doomed," too, her "melting comb" a bold figurative destruction of human memory and history held in the communal home.

But if the poem performs catastrophe, it does not end there. The razing has been in the service of another vision. In the final stanza Meehan employs a familiar trope in her poems, that of the shapeshifter, as the speaker, now both human female and bear, awaits the male bear lover. Long taken with such interspecies unions in myth and legend, Meehan says that the interest was awakened by her time in the Pacific Northwest when she was a graduate student at Eastern Washington University: "In the New World I came across many animal groom, animal bride stories, and a central story told by many of the first Nations peoples was the woman who married a bear. Every culture if you trace back holds in memory this idea of intercourse, of profound conversation between the humans and animals" (*Imaginary Bonnets* 48). For Meehan, such stories are valuable because

they hold in memory, like wings in amber, both original energies of and a template for, should we choose to avail ourselves of it, a wise and codependent relationship to the wild and to each other in community. It would be delusional to think that they might save us as we stand on this brink of global extinction but the hard

won vision may offer a clue to a saner, lighter tread on the earth.
Our only hope is a change of mind. (*Imaginary Bonnets* 48)

That change of mind appears in "The Solace of Artemis" as a
human narrator transformed during the course of the poem into
a female polar bear, who awaits perhaps this time a roving male
brown bear, the process of survival begun in another direction.
At the liminal threshold of the cave mouth, the narrator positions herself betwixt and between, that potent site of transformation, and imagines her cubs into another future. Those cubs,
"smelling of snow," maintain some aspects of their polar bear
mother but also, as "honied ones," possess qualities of their
brown bear father. With "sweet oblivion," Meehan gives us an
oxymoron that evokes both the surrender of a separate self to the
anticipated coupling but also the coming loss of an old identity
in a hybrid species whose survival is sweet. Like the premodern
peoples who took animal totems, belonged to animal clans, followed animal guides, and saw shape-shifting as a way of taking
on animal powers, Meehan suggests that if we attend to the other
animals, perhaps it is not we who will save them but they who
might instead save us.

THE LONGER, WIDER RIVER
In his introduction to Meehan's second Poetry Professor of
Ireland Lecture at Trinity College Dublin in November 2014,
Nicholas Grene observed that Meehan had done what Irish play-
wright John Synge was told by W. B. Yeats to do: express a life
that had never before found expression in poetry. "This is a new
poetry in Ireland. There ha[s] never been anything like this before."
But Grene also acknowledged that the descriptor "working class
Dublin woman poet" leaves out features of Meehan's world-
ranging scope, influenced by wide travel, Buddhism, the U.S. Beat
poets, and the mythology of Greece: "She is not a Dublin poet, she
is not a women's poet, she is a tributary if you like to what she has
herself called the longer, wider river that is world poetry."

The confluence of river metaphors in Grene's description of Meehan's work is suggestive, and indeed, as if taking the hint, Meehan called her final Poetry Professor of Ireland lecture, given in Belfast in November 2015, "Planet Water." Unpacking that title alone gives us access to significant currents in Meehan's work. According to the *Oxford English Dictionary*, the word *planet* is defined as "any of various rocky or gaseous bodies that revolve around the sun, the denotative meaning depending here on one among others, the materiality of the planetary bodies in relation, these bodies roughly visible to the human eye." And included in the etymology of "planet" is an organismic worldview: each planet is also a living agent informing the magical realm of astrology, and thus their physical presence is coupled with a less visible influence: "any of these bodies regarded in terms of its supposed influence or quality in affecting persons, events, and natural phenomena." Astronomy meets astrology, and science meets myth—the physical bodies of Mercury, Venus, Earth, Mars, Jupiter, Neptune, Saturn, and Pluto might be said to be coupled with a controlling and fateful pattern of energy humans do not, cannot, control. That sense of agency appears, too, in an etymological trace in "planet" from the second-century Greek and later the Latin: to "wander," "wanderer," and even "to lead astray." Thus, "Planet Water" gives us an active and animate natural world on a cosmic scale, evoking currents running throughout Meehan's poetry, from the omen of the geese in their flying formation in *Reading the Sky* to the palpable responses to space in the wide, horizontal branches of "The Wolf Tree" in *Painting Rain*.

In "Planet Water" the sense of one planet among others is coupled with our own planet's uniqueness, at least for us. The *OED* tells us that the phrase "planet earth" appeared in the mid- nineteenth century, at about the time when humans of the Industrial Revolution began to let loose the first loads of carbon that would bring us to our knees in the face of climate crisis today. The phrase "planet earth" singled out our own planet as among but distinct from the rest, and today we also associate the phrase with that first human view of ourselves as apart from the earth in the 1972 image of the earth seen from space by Apollo 17. With "Planet Water," Meehan also means to allude to our own earth engulfed by the water released by melting ice in Greenland and Antarctica, the rising temperatures of the oceans that will see several meters of sea level rise by the end of this century and the loss of many coastal cities. Thus, in her title alone, Meehan gives us her characteristic layers of resonance, her productive poetic ambiguity, and an anti-Cartesian view of a living, responding nature suffused with spirit.

A TRIBUTARY, IF YOU LIKE

The tributary Meehan's work supplies to the river of world poetry is precisely the embodying of the world itself. *World* from a Germanic word meaning "age of man" in the *OED* has, compared to "planet," a distinctly anthropocentric charge. From the twelfth century, it has meant "the state or realm of *human* existence on earth" or an era of human history. Even in its contrasts, the word *world* relies on human societies, as in "world of the afterlife" or "otherworld." Either entirely human or entirely not, the word "world" can in its overarching sense of being everything include a "planet or more or less celestial earthlike object" or "any part of the universe" or even "the earth and everything on it, the globe; the human environment; the countries of the earth collectively." But these meanings are vastly outnumbered by an etymological focus on all things human, and even in these we come back to the environment where humans find themselves and the countries they have constructed.

We might say that "planet" re-earths the "world" of "world literature" or at least the theory of world literature, which remains profoundly anthropocentric. Leading theorists of world literature, David Damrosch, Franco Moretti, and Pascale Casanova, are variously concerned with world literary systems, the focus entirely on relationships between human cultures, national literatures, and literary markets. Is world literature "the symphony of masterpieces from different nations" or the "global distribution of books as commodities" (Thomsen 13)? Is a literature defined as "world" because it has inspired universal interest across time and space? Damrosch argues that "international circulation and an impact on other cultures is essential" to any literature called world" (Thomsen 15) while Moretti maintains that the presence of the metropolitan and colonizing *core* alongside a rural (read undeveloped) and colonized *periphery* is a defining feature (34). For Casanova the focus is on the functioning of the international literary field itself, where despite the disadvantages writers of smaller nations face, some do manage to change the world literary system from the periphery (Thomsen 18). None of these views is irrelevant to a discussion of Meehan as a writer of poetry; Moretti's definition of world literature might include much of the Irish literary canon, Meehan's work along with it. Certainly, in Casanova's formulation, Meehan has moved from a peripheral social class within Ireland itself to a position of influence among Irish poets and increasingly among poets of other nation-states as well. It remains to be seen whether writing from what Damrosch calls the "counter-canon" "composed of the subaltern and contestatory voices of writers in less commonly-taught languages and in minor literatures within great-power languages" (qtd. in Thomsen 18), Meehan's work will change the world literature canon, contested as it is. To adapt Marx, these theorists have *interpreted* world literature in various ways. The point for Meehan is to *change* what we mean by the "world" itself.

PLANETARY POETICS

The distinctions I've discussed could convince us that "world" may not be an apt term for the kind of poet Meehan is, for her "world" is not an entirely human one, not by any means. Indeed, I'd want to call hers a planetary poetics, a "planetary" rather than a "world" literary prose. Jody Allen Randolph has identified in Meehan's work a "planetary imaginary" (qtd. in Villar-Argaíz 182) and Pilar Villar-Argaíz has discussed Meehan's "planetary consciousness" as "a way of thinking which extends beyond parochial interests to incorporate the whole biosphere" (182). Yet the meaning and import of *planetarity* is not only much debated, it may remain so. Gayatri Spivak observes of the vastness of this perspective, "I cannot offer a formulaic access to planetarity. No one can" (78). In "Climate and Capital: On Conjoined Histories," Dipesh Chakrabarty observes that the orientation of those working in the field of comparative planetary studies "is not human centered. It speaks to a growing divergence in our consciousness between the global—a singularly human story—and the planetary, a perspective to which humans are incidental. The climate crisis is about waking up to the rude shock of the planet's otherness" (23). In this formulation, Chakrabarty builds on Spivak's contention that "[t]he planet is the species of alterity, belonging to another system; and yet we inhabit it, on loan. It is not really amenable to a neat contrast with the globe" (Spivak 72). Amy Elias and Christian Moraru concur: a planetary perspective moves us from "globe as financial-technocratic system toward planet as world ecology" (xvi). *Planetarity* becomes "a move away from the totalizing paradigm of modern-age globalization" (xi) toward a "new structure of awareness" involving "relatedness, dialogue, and interactivity" as well as new "forms of 'self-other' interplay" (xii). Moreover, "*planetarity* opens itself to the nonhuman, the organic, and the inorganic in all their richness" (xxiii). Yet while Elias and Moraru align humans with a stewardship role in world ecology, Meehan's work leans more toward a partnership ethic with reciprocity and exchange as central. In this way I would argue that Meehan works to imaginatively map an alternative human subjectivity by exploring planetary otherness. In dialogue with the nonhuman, her work takes its cues from the elements and models humility in the face of forces of nature.

In "Planet Water," the sounds of water and the movement of the river teach Meehan how to speak. Take this example of poetic prose from early in "Planet Water." Having opened the scene of the writing of this lecture with "rain bucketing from the heavens" and then following that water through "the underground drainage arteries into the rivers, and finally into the sea from where it will lift again into the clouds," Meehan characterizes the lecture itself and all it contains as embarking on various kinds of voyages, the literal ones inseparable from the metaphoric:

> For this journey I need the language of water, a tongue that can speak in river vowels, in the glottal stops of rapids, a language turned in the great tides and braided on the shores of the world, the music of floods and calving glaciers, the deep-delved riffs of springs and wells, the melodies of beck and brook and burn, the harmonics of rain and tarn and lake, snow tunes, ice tunes, ballads wrought of drizzle and mizzle, the low lying estuarial land of Baldoyle where the River Moyne, locally pronounced Mayne, flows into the Irish sea. A small river, not much to look at, but it drains a huge area of north Dublin and irrigates the eel grass that is the staple winter feeding of our most distinctive visitors, the Brent Geese. (*Imaginary Bonnets* 55)

Having engaged in interspecies dialogue in the first two lectures, here Meehan gives us a narrator in intimate relation with the element of water. Her human narrator seeks the relationship, knowing that her subject "needs" this interchange, and we experience the interaction as readers in the swift currents of rhythm and rhyme, alliteration and assonance: the onomatopoetic plosives of "glottal stops of rapids" give way to the expansive and diffuse n's and long vowels of "language turned in the great tides" before leaping to the alliterative shifts of "beck and brook and burn" and the playful mist of "drizzle and mizzle," all the twists and turns connected in one long, flowing sentence that listens and has us listen to the being of water. But then the language turns matter of fact as the narrator informs us that although human aesthetics may not value the appearance of the River Moyne—"a small river, not much to look at"—in fact, the ecological services the river performs are myriad, exceeding all anthropomorphic expectations: the river "drains" and "irrigates" so that eel grass grows and Brent geese are in their migrations fed. The narrator's expanded, planetary awareness has, on many levels, taken it all in; we might be transformed in our ecological awareness and values in equal measure. This is what Elias and Moraru have described as the ethical dimension of planetarity, though Meehan's partnership ethic neither absents nor privileges the presence of human beings. Rather, her perspective suggests that the planet and its creatures have as much if not more to offer than the human, and human beings might become truly exceptional by relinquishing the belief that they are.

Later in "Planet Water," Meehan's narrator joins the Brent geese in a dream, shape-shifting like Angus Og in the Irish legend: "I was cruising in the wake of the leading bird, knowing in my goose brain that I was heading for Stangford Lough. I felt very happy as part of the flock, enjoying the tension of the wind in my feathers, the bird's eye view of the beautiful Antrim coastline" (*Imaginary Bonnets* 69). Just as the narrators of her poems shape-shift into a dressed deer in "Instructions to the Absent Husband" or a polar bear in "The Solace of Artemis," here Meehan changes her human skin for an animal one. The borders of the body and the borders of the state are crossed and recrossed just as later in the essay, a poem is crossed with the tarot spread and the natural with the supernatural. In "Planet Water" the human narrator crosses the Atlantic to drink water in the kitchen of twentieth-century poet Elizabeth Bishop's Nova Scotia kitchen and recite Bishop's poem "Sestina" in another room of the house where poster poems by Eavan Boland and Seamus Heaney hang from the walls. Describing an existential crisis in her sixtieth year, Meehan takes us through a dramatic tarot reading during which she both experiences a vision and emerges profoundly changed.

It's instructive here to return as Meehan does to one of her own touchstones, a poem she has often referred to as a guiding text, Gary Snyder's "What You Should Know to Be a Poet." Indeed, Snyder's poem grounds this lecture as it has grounded Meehan herself throughout her writing life. The injunctions in Snyder's "What You Should Know to Be a Poet" are, I would argue, an early manifesto for a planetary poetics: "all you can know about animals as persons. / the names of trees and the movements of planets and the moon. /. . . . / at least one kind of traditional magic" (*Imaginary Bonnets* 60). The specificity of all life in this injunction, one Meehan has taken to heart throughout her writing life, widens the frame on what counts as subjects for poetry. The connections here among flora, fauna, celestial bodies, and multiple ways of knowing are all elements of a planetary poetics. Like Yeats before her, Meehan's work pushes back at the limits modernity has placed on human experience and imports significant elements of the premodern. In this view, the writing of poetry itself becomes a form of scrying: "The poem is reading you as the spread is reading you, reading where you come from, what you bring to it, your education, your tolerance, your ear, your heartbeat, your experience, your insight, your vocabulary, your history, and your understanding of your history" (*Imaginary Bonnets* 73). Skeptical of human hyperrationality, Meehan here as elsewhere models a reciprocity with an animate material world where the poet both makes the poem and is made by it. Poetry itself becomes a powerful tool of divination, a way of cultivating what Snyder describes as the "watchful and elegant mind." Far from separating Meehan from an embodied experience of the material world, the stance fosters engagement on every level. Her lecture finally winds back to an immediate political response to water:

> I recite the poem now as a spell against the Frackers, the energy companies who want to extract the natural gas from the shale that underlies the whole of our beautiful lake district, Fermanagh and Leitrim, under the land and under the lakes, where our bounteous aquifers are. The process risks poisoning the wells, it will be impossible to prevent the toxic residues from entering the water table, from polluting the aquifers. The river doesn't recognize the border,

the lakes do not recognize the border, the underground aquifers
for sure don't recognize the border. (*Imaginary Bonnets* 75)

Here the magic, the spell, of the poem is in the service of the element. The precious water that the mechanistic mindset of global
capitalism threatens to render toxic is given a voice. Unafraid
of public protest, Meehan has used each of her lectures as Poetry
Professor of Ireland to address poetry's role in an era of global
climate change. Refusing to speak the language of the earth
and engage in dialogue with a living planet, the energy companies profit from the mechanistic worldview of modernity, where
nature is viewed as dead matter for instrumental use. And Meehan
puts the problem in a global context by making visible the Irish
movement protesting fracking, Shell to Sea, and making the link
with another poet across time and space, Nigerian Ken Saro-Wiwa:
"Our underwater resources have been made over to a gang who
have the blood of a Nigerian novelist and poet on their hands"
(*Imaginary Bonnets* 75). This, too, is a planetary poetics, a poetry
that troubles the borders of nation-states. It is poetry that rubs
elbows with poetry of other nations—influencing and open to influence. It sits beside poetry from other regions, other continents,
other states in world literature anthologies. Dug into the local, it
has made its way across borders so that its craft and its content are
meaningful to readers beyond its national borders. Its audience is
broader than the local though rooted in the local. Meehan's poetry
crosses all these boundaries in order to explore new futures beyond
the limits of neoliberal nation-states and human exceptionalism.

INTERVIEW

HOWTH HEAD, SUMMER 2014

PAULA MEEHAN: If you follow the coast, you see there's a stone wall. Well, you might have to get out to see it, where the inlet turns. I'm just in there in a small house in a small housing section. So that's how far or near I am from here.

KATHRYN KIRKPATRICK: And what do you call that district?

PM: Baldoyle. It's "Baile Dubh Gall": the town of the dark-haired stranger. But it's in a bigger area, this whole area stretching right up the coast northwards and around is called Fingal, which is the "territory of the fair-haired stranger," "Finn-Gall." This fair stranger would be the Norse, Vikings, first came the Vikings and then later the Danes, the dark-haired strangers. And Dublin was founded as a city by the Danes with its own currency, with King Sitric's head on the coinage.

KK: So how do you think about your ancestry?

PM: Well, how far back do you want to go? Let's start from the Bronze Age, the Milesians really, the small dark people. We drove the Tuatha Dé Danann, the tall, fair, elvish people, underground into the raths. So that's what I think of my ancestry! I'm from a family that is part Dublin, but our roots go back into West Cork, the McCarthys. My mother was a McCarthy, my grandfather was a McCarthy, a crafts-man who did mosaic work and tiled floors, mainly in the churches of the city. There's a strong craftwork tradition in the McCarthys. So I have roots going back through Cork city into West Cork, a territory I adore, the very ground of it. And I get there any chance I can. The other side of the family, Meehan, is from Leitrim originally. It's up northwest, and we were a small sect under the protection of the McGuires. I think we came into Dublin about the time of the famine.

My great-grandmother Anna was the last of the madames, in the Monto, at the turn of the nineteenth into the twentieth century, the biggest red-light district in Europe. They say that everyone in Monto has royal blood in them, you know, so who knows what my ancestry is! Like most island people I'm a mongrel. The part of me that's from the heart of the city and the part of the city I spent my childhood in, I relish. It's the place that I got language first. It's a place and a community that I'm committed to, you know. I love the people, their spirit of survival against unbearable odds. And it is also part of the city where the new Irish are finding a foothold, on top of an already pressured community. But the community, and especially the community leaders, who have always been visionary and quite antiauthoritarian really, they made space and they developed projects, community projects, especially through the arts and through sports that embraced the newcomers. The schools of the area are working really hard to promote integration, you know, really holistic integration. It is quite marvelous, and it's always under threat, these most important civilizing projects, civilizing *us* to the potential of otherness in our communities. But, you know, I just see, everywhere I go, I see really heroic volunteers even in conditions of economic collapse where we've become like a slave nation financially to some actually quite sinister idea of centralized power—the new empire—and we've been screwed by the bankers.

KK: It's just appalling the Citizens United [a court ruling in the United States], you know, that corporations can give any amount of money to campaigns. Disaster.

PM: All I can offer to the situation as a citizen is poetry. Poems, like dreams, can be messages—deep, deep messages—from the self to the frontal lobes and can show us direction, show us healing, show us understanding, if we can get far enough out of our own way to be open to them. The poems have agency in the world, I believe, and they're woven in and out of all our individual little scenes or nets of survival, our poetry communities. They are gifts to be given out and shared.

KK: They put things to rest sometimes too. They exorcise things in a way.

PM: John McGahern, the great Irish novelist (and the first workshop I did was with McGahern, you know, the first purely literary workshop), he would say that publication was a way of burying your dead. And he also said something I thought was very, very interesting, that you should measure yourself by the grandeur of your failures, rather than by your accomplishments or success. He thought it was a waste of everyone's time if you didn't have this constant push forward as an artist. Otherwise, you know, why would you bother?

KK: When I studied Keats, that's what I noticed. He would try the most ambitious, wild, "Endymion," these poetic experiments that didn't entirely work. And then he'd fall back and write the gorgeous odes. He'd been stretched by the failures.

PM: Oh, yes, I think we have to write a lot of bad poetry. If you're remembered by four or five poems, well, fantastic, you know. That tentative and very, very vulnerable thing that is our shared memory: living memory in some communities is long-lived, and in the poetry community, living memory goes back a long way. But I would hate to see living memory in the poetry community confined to written-down memory. I think our remit is far older and longer-tailed, that actually writing is just a technological phase the poetry is going through as it works through us, her humble servants, and wears us out.

KK: Where's it going to be in the digital age?

PM: Well, it's already happening and it's hard to catch it because I think after a certain age as a poet, you are absolutely involved with what Yeats called the quarrel with yourself. And it's both a relief and a challenge. "Where is it going to be in the digital age?" is not my question. I would write the poems now that I have to write. I'm into my end game in some kind of strange way, and I feel that is just fabulous because I absolutely write the poems I have to write. Isn't that great? And you know, I don't care. It's a lovely kind of liberation in the last few years, maybe the last decade, moving through all kinds of phases of change and loss.

KK: Your work is a very profound record of, besides everything else, the trip and the journey. I've learned an awful lot from it. I understand that some of it is my own projection, but still. Every critic does it.

PM: I assume you're talking about learning from your own work. We do learn from our own work, don't we?

KK: Yes, but also I'm learning from yours. You know, the journey I've found in your poems, or projected onto your poems. You never know.

PM: I've done some dream training with my good friend, a Dublin woman, Juliet Clancy. She's an extraordinary dream worker. I've done poetry and dream workshops with her, comoderated them. And she works with the dream in a way that I've found very helpful for working with the poem. It takes the poem out of the narrowly critical hands for the students, even though I suppose the critical hands might not even really exist. They are probably projections—you know, the critic on the shoulder.

KK: I'd like to go to that workshop sometime.

PM: We did it three times. A residential week in a beautiful setting in West Cork. And I had her come and teach the techniques to some of the community groups I worked with because it's simply a very useful, and safe, way of exploring the self. I had found that out anyway before I invited Juliet in, certainly in the community I come from and in the projects I sometimes go back to work in. Dreams. It's a great basis on which start a poetry workshop: "What did you dream last night?" "Isn't that strange? Isn't that a strange

FIGURE 1 The author with Paula Meehan at Aideen's Grave on Howth Head, 2014. Photo by author.

image?" "Let's get some of this down." "Let's start from here with these stories that our minds are telling to ourselves." We start there, and we listen to each other's dreams. Such a totally natural way into what our own image making and what our own faculties have to offer.

KK: And respectful. There are some people who regard dreams as just trash. And that's such a loss, isn't it?

PM: I think that we can learn to dream. We can practice the dream. And Juliet taught me that sometimes we carry dreams for others, we dream for our communities. And when we voice the dream, whoever's there to hear it, it might be their own dream they're hearing, that we have carried for them. So that was a radical new piece of information for me in the last few years. It's probably eight years since we did the workshops, and I'm still reverberating out of it. I had just taught poetry as a craft. That's all I do in the workshops. I just concentrate on craft as a way of having something to talk about. But what one tradition of practice had to show the other was obvious. We didn't have to label it. I think that it's only reaffirmed what I've felt instinctively all my life.

6

THE SHAMANIC POET

———

In a discussion of Yeats's magical influence on poet Ted Hughes, Rand Brandes observes that critics have shied away from "the earliest and most sustained significant point of contact between these poets. It was Yeats as shaman in his early poem 'The Wanderings of Oisin' that first caught Hughes's attention and held it, and when Hughes looked to Yeats throughout his life, he looked to 'The Wanderings of Oisin' for guidance and assurance" (198). For indications of how Meehan arrives at the "earth magic" of *Geomantic* (2016), we might substitute in the passage above Gary Snyder for Yeats, Meehan for Hughes, and Snyder's poem "What You Should Know to Be a Poet" for "The Wanderings of Oisin." And this would not be to ignore similarities between Meehan's and Yeats's perspectives. If "The Wanderings of Oisin" "records Yeats's visionary call to magic out of a Bardic tradition rooted in Druidic shamanism" (Brandes 199), Meehan's "One Evening in May" might be said to serve as a similar visionary call.

I discussed the profound influence of Snyder's writing, and "What You Should Know to Be a Poet," in particular, on Meehan and her work in chapter 3. Here I take up the risky business of situating her poems in the tradition of Western magic's influence on poetry. Though Meehan chose to omit "One Evening in May" from her later volume of selected poems, even the title to that volume, *As If By Magic* (2020), playfully names the rhizome of magical consciousness informing her work. I am not arguing that Meehan is a practicing magician or shaman who systematically applies magic in her life, and I'm not aware of any formal system of symbols of the kind Yeats devised informing her poems. Indeed, unlike Yeats, Meehan is not a poet of master narratives or master plans. Her narrators display a receptive humility in the presence of the otherness of the more-than-human rather than an embrace of magic in the classical sense of "manipulating forces or beings to some instrumental end" (Giesler 209). What I *am* suggesting is that the trajectory of Meehan's work issues a striking challenge to modernity's delimiting of the ways we understand the world. Part of that challenge involves a serious engagement with alternative ways of knowing what we might call a magical state of mind as well as the practice of shape-shifting peculiar to shamanism.

MODERNITY'S REPRESSED OTHER

In her discussion of Western theories of magic, environmental historian Carolyn Merchant describes the Neoplatonic magic of the Renaissance as an enabling tradition for the mechanistic worldview it helped to usher in: the Scientific Revolution of the sixteenth and seventeenth centuries in Europe. Neoplatonic magic assumed a hierarchical universe with passive and subordinate matter (or the world body) linked to the "world soul" by the animating force of the *spiritus mundi* (*Death of Nature* 106–7): "Operating within this hierarchy, the magus would draw down the celestial powers to marry inferiors to superiors, and therefore to manipulate nature for individual benefit. . . . The Renaissance magus as an operator and arranger of natural objects became the basis of a new optimism that nature could be altered for human progress" (109). The magus's intimacy with the elements helped him to vanquish nature as he (not she) elevated "himself above the angels . . . with whom he then becomes cooperator and can do all things" (109). By retaining this hierarchical view of the universe but rejecting earlier beliefs in the organismic and animistic aspects of matter, the Scientific Revolution, and its attendant colonial pursuits, could then sanction the scientific investigation of and colonial extraction from an earth now figured as dead.

But Neoplatonic magic became a casualty of the scientific worldview it enabled, and with it the magician, who no longer had credible celestial forces to command. The control of a disenchanted and empirically knowable nature was now the business of scientists. What continues into modernity, if in subterranean form, is, as Amitav Ghosh has described it, the alternative magical tradition of vitalism, "the belief that spirit existed in all matter" (86). Introduced into Europe by Paracelsus, the fifteenth-century alchemist, physician, and philosopher, vitalism continues the premodern conception of a living earth, imbued with agency. In Paracelsus's holistic cosmology, the astral spirit, which originated in the stars, and is "the source of divinity in all sublunar life, including animals, plants, minerals, and stones," is also located in the human heart and forms "the imaginative faculty joining the physical with the spiritual worlds" (Merchant, *Death of Nature* 119). This vital substance imbuing all things thus allows humans "to create visible images of the astra through the application of art" (119) and affect even the source of the astra itself. In this conception of a living earth known, in part, through the imagination, the poet clearly has a consequential role.

The English Romantic poets were among those who kept alive a vitalist understanding of the world even as the mechanistic and scientific view of the earth made possible the Industrial Revolution and the colonial plunder that fueled it. Moreover, Alison Butler suggests that having taken his visionary guidance from one of the Romantics, William Blake, Yeats worked with the secret magical order of the late 19th and early 20th century, the Golden Dawn, to reanimate the imagination as a balance to modernity's "scientific empiricism" (226). For Butler, this was part of the Golden Dawn's recasting of magic from a power over nature and a focus on the will of the magician toward the development of "the magician's spirit to a more enlightened state in which the individual's powers of perception and intuition are heightened and access is gained to higher powers" (222). Although Western magical genealogies are not the only traditions from which Meehan's work draws, her insistent evocation of an animate natural world carries forward an explicit poetic tradition of contact with what Ghosh has called "the subterranean tide of vitalism that has lived on through the ages as modernity's repressed Other" (241). However, in Meehan's work the personal enlightenment of the poet through heightened powers of perception and intuition also serves a larger communal purpose, and one that connects her work more broadly to the practices of shamans.

"WHAT ARE YOU LOOKING AT, WITCH?"

Gender, class, and ecology come together as a vitalist triumvirate in the figure of the witch. Usually female, often from the lower classes, and associated with both animal familiars and spells drawn from the energies of the earth, witches were subjected to the violence directed toward all those who, in Ghosh's words, held "improper views of nature":

> The modern conception of matter as inert—or "as an inanimate object of inquiry"—emerged out of several intersecting processes of violence: between Catholics and Protestants; between various Protestant sects; between elite European men and poor women; and perhaps most significantly, between European colonizers and Indigenous peoples of the Americas, many of whom believed that earthly forces and material entities of all kinds had innate powers and agency. The struggle over these diametrically opposed views was a metaphysical conflict that mirrored the violence of the terrestrial wars that were then being fought between settlers and natives. The aim of eradicating "the belief that spirit existed in all matter" thus came at the "final stage of English conquest-over nature, and over those who had improper views of nature." (86–87)

Ghosh's conjoining of apparently disparate groups targeted because of a common belief in a vitalist worldview accords with feminist historian Silvia Federici's discussion of the great witch hunt of the sixteenth and seventeenth centuries. Unfolding during the rise of the Scientific Revolution, the witch hunt also coincided with the defeat of the European peasantry (Federici, *Caliban* 63), among whom dwelt "popular healers, sorcerers, and magicians, whose magical procedures had resulted from many years of transmitting verbal recipes and cures handed down from medieval and ancient times" (Merchant, *Death of Nature* 121). With the expulsion of these peasants from the source of their livelihood, common land, a way of life informed by vitalist systems was displaced. In this context, a world proletariat of dispossessed laborers and enslaved Native Americans and Africans was forced to forge the colonial era: "The process required the transformation of the body into a work-machine, and the subjection of women to the reproduction of the work-force. Most of all, it required the destruction of the power of women which, in Europe as in America, was achieved through the extermination of the 'witches'" (Federici, *Caliban* 63).

Uniquely positioned as targets, witches were among those thought to hold "improper views of nature." Associated with nature's disorderly aspects, these women with knowledge and power were considered a threat. Already regarded as closer to nature because more closely associated with the body, women, Federici observes, were identified with "a degraded conception of corporeal reality" (*Caliban* 15). Of the tens of thousands of women charged with the crime of witchcraft during this tumultuous period, from forty thousand to sixty thousand are believed to have been executed (Russell).

The specter of disorderly women with magical powers emerges in Meehan's sequence of poems "A Change of Life" in *Painting Rain*. Here I call back to my reading of "Scrying" in chapter 3 with added resonance. Having long drawn on her witchy working-class female relatives to fully inhabit her eclectically constructed role of poet seer, in "Scrying" Meehan represents the targeting of a witch amid the social upheaval of the Celtic Tiger era when the sudden influx of wealth rent Ireland's social fabric.

The stars have a purple glow and the red
devil of desire is jerking our strings:
we are avid puppets in his hands.

Enslaved by money and the lure of power
we rattle our talismans. Our dance,
if we have one anymore, is under

the baton of St. Vitus, millennial, macabre.
This new fever has a grip on the island
and everyone wants, wants, wants

more space, more grace, more avoirdupois
wandering around with our lower material selves
hanging out—like that boy the other day

near the dying chestnuts at the station
who, shaking his penis at me, screamed
What are you looking at witch? (*PR* 62–63)

Federici has observed that the sundering of the kinship and
community ties of collective land-tenure systems helped create the
societal divisions and complicity with the state that made witch
hunts possible (*Caliban* 171). Just so, in Meehan's poem the Celtic
Tiger's exacerbation of the uneven distribution of wealth fuels
discord. Recolonized by capital, the country and its citizens have
lost their agency, puppets lured and enslaved by an insatiable
desire for material plenty. In the prosody of the poem, greed and
excess show up as the repetition of desire: *wants, wants, wants,
more, more, more.* Unrhymed tercets mostly break grammatical
sentences across stanzas: there's not much connected or contained
here. The social body's fever is figured as disorder of the physical
body, the St. Vitus' dance mirrored in the boy's shaking penis. The
poem both inhabits the authentic identity of the witch who predicts through her scrying an unbalanced future and also represents

the aggression of the unhinged boy who has made her the target of the destructive forces she identifies. Yet it is the community to which the boy belongs that the poem works to right through writing and witness, and later in the sequence Meehan celebrates marginalized members of this community by revivifying the traditions of the Travelers, their vitalistic practices and worldview. Thus, in "Sweeping the Garden," the witchy narrator describes her friendship with the resettled Traveler child Bertie, whose "cultured beautiful mind" (*PR* 64) and lively premodern perspective are missed by her standard-issue schooling. In this sequence of poems, Meehan rescues the figure of the witch in order to exorcise its degraded aspects in favor of another kind of knowing. For this a wider, more capacious conception of magic and a magical state of mind is needed, one including but not limited to purely Western conceptions.

A MAGICAL STATE OF MIND

Anthropologist Susan Greenwood emphasizes the experiential aspects of "[a] magical 'state of mind' as having an intrinsically subjective and sensory quality that is embodied and intuitive rather than purely reflective and intellectual, although the reflective and intellectual may be engaged *with* the intuitive and the embodied as there is no radical opposition" (7). Like Yeats's description of the poet as possessing "passionate intellect," Greenwood's formulation moves beyond the Cartesian dualisms of reason and feeling or mind and body, opening up "consciousness as a process that is inclusive of the body as well as . . . other beings in nature and even perhaps being an intrinsic quality of a wider universe" (6). Both a practitioner of magic and a scholar of magic, Greenwood argues for magical consciousness as a legitimate and compatible way of knowing that works analogically "with divergent forms of feeling, creates patterns, is very participatory, and makes connections between spirit and matter" (Parmigiani). Though all cultures "have both forms of thinking and knowing" (Parmigiani), contemporary practitioners of nature religions, especially in the West, explicitly seek to build bridges between logical and analogical ways of knowing and thereby rebalance an overvaluing of the former and an undervaluing of the latter. Just so, geophilosopher David Abram suggests that "[i]f we wish to renew our solidarity with the more-than-human terrain, then we may need to think in some fresh ways" (130). Ecofeminist philosopher Val Plumwood concurs: "We need a thorough and open rethink which has the courage to question our most basic cultural narratives" ("Active Voice" 41). For Abram these fresh ways of knowing involve reframing psychology as transpersonal and the human mind as one among others, capable of meeting with "other minds in oak, fir, hawk, snake, stone, rain, and salmon," because "all aspects of place make up a particular state of mind" (262). For both of these environmental philosophers, modernist conceptions of the autonomous, rational human subject are woefully inadequate and incomplete.

Attending to the voices of the more-than-human world is central to Amitav Ghosh's reframing of the writer's task in our era of climate crisis: "What does it mean to live on Earth as though it were Gaia—that is to say, a living, vital entity in which many kinds of beings tell stories?" (205). For Ghosh, recognizing the uncanny in human experience is one way of acknowledging the agency of a living earth. He takes among his inspirations the Yanomami shaman Davi Kopenawa whose memoir and "compendium of knowledge," *The Falling Sky,* witnesses to the ravages of settler-colonial terraforming of his homeland, Brazil's Amazonas province (206). Through the use of the mind-altering bark of the *yākoana hi* tree, Yanomami shamans learn to enter the inspirited world of all beings—"humans, animals, trees, water, plants" (206). Kopenawa's capacity to commune with the *xapiri,* the spirits of nature, leads him beyond "the binomial names of the Linnean system" (209); "the forest far exceeds human comprehension; a name given by humans to a tree would not even begin to exhaust its presence in the world . . . the *xapiri* are the true owners of 'nature,' not human beings" (209). For Yanomami, "a shaman's work is to protect the earth" (qtd. in Ghosh 206). For Ghosh, writers and artists who include the voices of the nonhuman in their writing are central to that protection. And such nonhuman stories can only be told by those willing to transform their own modernist conceptions of the human.

In these terms, the boundary-crossing sensibility I have been charting in Meehan's writing becomes part of an enriching expansion of modern Western rationalism such that logical and empirical epistemologies are augmented by analogical and participatory states of mind. Thus, in Meehan's "The Solace of Artemis," the tools of science uncover an ancient ursine story that the narrator imaginatively enters by shape-shifting with a polar bear. Later, in Meehan's essay "Planet Water," the narrator delivers ecological knowledge of the River Moyne alongside her joyful transformation through dream into one of the significant visitors to that habitat, a Brent goose: "I felt very happy as part of the flock, enjoying the tension of the wind in my feathers, the bird's eye view of the beautiful Antrim coastline" (*Imaginary Bonnets* 69). Greenwood calls this shape-shifting a form of "participatory consciousness," and she, too, has shared a state of mind with a bird, hers an owl, with whom she felt so merged in trance that, like Meehan, she could feel the wind in the feathers of her wings (Parmigiani): "It's that connection with the nonhuman world . . . that I feel is so important today in terms of our ecological crisis. Because [other animals] become more like kin, and they have messages for us if we'll listen" (Parmigiani).

SHAMANISM

If the use of the term *shaman* seems portentous and culturally appropriating in the context of modern and contemporary poetry, it's important to remember that Meehan has always taken the long view of the role of the poet. In her interview with Jody Allen Randolph in *Close to the Next Moment*, Meehan observes that the first written mention of a poet in Ireland was Amergin, poet of the Milesian invaders, whose song derived from the oral traditions of the Irish bards of the Bronze Age. Amergin acknowledges the origins of his poem in the otherworld of the Sidhe: "I will go to the

rath of the Sidhe . . . to meet the poet, that together we can con-
coct a powerful incantation" (34). Here Meehan frames poetry as
magical speech, a spell with the power to make something happen.
Derived from the coming together of the Indigenous and the other
in the otherworld, the origins of poems emerge as transpersonal
and transspecies. The "Song of Amergin" becomes "this wonderful
piece of transpersonal identification and being with the landscape
and creatures—'I am a wind of the sea, I am a wave of the sea, I am
the stag of seven tines, I am a salmon in a pool'—that utterance of
the landscape, almost an aboriginal calling of the landscape into
being" (Allen Randolph, *Next Moment* 33).

In his founding text of the anthropological study of shamanism, Mircea Eliade suggests that many conventions of the epic, including subjects, motifs, characters, and images, are "of ecstatic
origin, in the sense that they were borrowed from the narratives
of shamans describing their journeys and adventures in the super-
human worlds" (510). Likewise, Eliade draws close links between
shamanic practice and lyric poetry:

> In preparing his trance, the shaman drums, summons his spirit
> helpers, speaks a "secret language" or the "animal language,"
> imitating the cries of beasts and especially the songs of birds. He
> ends by obtaining a "second state" that provides the impetus for
> linguistic creation and the rhythms of lyric poetry. Poetic cre-
> ation still remains an act of perfect spiritual freedom. (510)

This mystical merging with the living world of nature is figured
as "negotiations with the Goddess" by Ted Hughes in this charac-
terization of the poet as shaman: "The essential experience of the
Shaman is purely psychic, a magical flight to the Goddess, and a
return to worldliness with something divine, a cure, an inspired
answer, some kind of blessing everybody recognizes" (Brandes 202).
This poet is "pre-historic" and her deity is a "Nature/Goddess with
drum, dance and song—entranced and ecstatic" (204). Just so,
Snyder's "What You Must Know to Be a Poet" concludes by wishing

the poet both the externalized delights of "extasy" in the "wild freedom of the dance" as well as the internal delights of "enstasy" in "silent solitary illumination" (*Regarding Wave* 40). Moreover, in all these magical conceptions of the poet's role, Meehan's included, the healing of the community is central, and this healing comes about through the "power of magically animated imagination" (Brandes 209). As Meehan puts this in "She-Who-Walks-Among-The-People," "She went to the courts / of the island and fought for the women there / with her marvellous gift of speech" (*PT* 61).

In his charting of the shamanic in contemporary poetry, Shamasad Mortuza acknowledges that both modernist poets of the occult and more recent "shamanic" poets have a common bardic origin in the pre-Christian priestly caste of Druids, seers who carried "the whole culture of the people" (22): "The acceptance of the shaman as an alter-ego for the poet was helped by the fact that for centuries, the offices of the poets have been linked to prophets, priests, shamans, bards, medicine-men, seers, visionaries, oracle bringers, culture heroes, helpers, tricksters, magicians, and the outsiders. The cultural memory helped the growth of the shaman as an aesthetic category" (25).

Poet Jerome Rothenberg bridges "the ethnographic and literary shaman through what he calls ethnopoetics" (Mortuza 28), an idea he shares with Gary Snyder in which the ritualistic use of language and sacred actions serve to cure, heal, and define reality in a meaningful way for oneself and the community (Mortuza 28). Moreover, shamanic poetry becomes efficacious through performance, both through the reader's participation in and engagement with the poem on the page (Mortuza 43) and also through the actual performance of the poem for audiences. Indeed, known for her distinctive, incantatory delivery of poems in person, Meehan has said that for her the public performance completes the full arc of a poem's reach in the world.

Mortuza, however, makes necessary distinctions between the engagement with the occult of high modernist poets like Yeats, Eliot, and Pound and a contemporary shamanic poetics. He describes the latter as late modernist, a "radical poetic practice" that maintains the link with a modernist past but with a difference: "Late modernist poetics is essentially curative and in search of an alternative mode of expression while leaving behind the reactionary politics of high modernists" (Mortuza 7). For Mortuza, late modernism is self-aware, incorporating a critique of the violence of colonialism and empire that have dominated and demonized the Other in order to accumulate wealth through colonial plunder. This radical poetic practice opposes "commodity-fetishism" and engages "in various experiments in art, with an urgency of social change" (8).

POETRY OF THE WORLD BEING ITSELF

In her third Poetry Professor of Ireland essay, "Planet Water," Meehan describes a shamanic journey inspired by a trip to Nova Scotia where she visits the childhood home of the great North American poet Elizabeth Bishop. Standing in the very kitchen that inspired Bishop's "Sestina," Meehan recites the poem into the kitchen itself, which she figures as "a sacred space, a temenos" (*Imaginary Bonnets* 56). In the context of what follows, the experience of visiting this homeplace as "temenos," as temple, is akin to Hughes's "negotiation with the goddess." Soon after, on the threshold of returning home across the ocean to Ireland, Meehan recounts a visit to a reader of animal tarot cards, an encounter that brings on that most shamanic of trances, flight as a bird. What follows is the sensation of "wind rushing through my feathers" (*Imaginary Bonnets* 57):

> I can feel myself soaring, it might be for hours or minutes, I cannot tell, then I am hanging in air a moment, then riding a thermal down and through the surface of a vast ocean and experiencing music, in a kind of hearing that happens on the body, on the skin itself, more pulse than sound maybe. I have no sense of human time. (*Imaginary Bonnets* 58)

This boundaryless synesthesia evokes Eliade's shamanic trance and Snyder's *enstasy*, the self birdlike, free from the human constructs of space and time. When Meehan returns to her human form, she is changed, conversant with the transpersonal and the transspecies, able to glimpse the span of human history and beyond, "the dreamtime of our species" (59). This dreamtime reveals the human "journey into self-consciousness, or even the geologic, and I would go so far as to say geomantic, time of our evolution, the script we read in fossils, petrified forests, read in a handful of soil, carried here and there by wayward, unseen rivers. The poetry of the world being itself" (*Imaginary Bonnets* 59).

The connections between the earth, the shaman, and the poet could hardly be more clear. Like Ghosh and the shaman Yanomami, the protection of the earth emerges as central when Meehan registers distress over "the dualistic and dangerous human sense of being separate from the rest of nature" (*Imaginary Bonnets* 59). The trance experience has reaffirmed the connections between poetry and the uncanny for Meehan, poetry and magic, and on her trip home she turns to the active clairvoyance of scrying: "The blank page as scrying medium. I am flying home, thirty-six thousand feet over the Atlantic Ocean, the blank page of my notebook invites me to scry" (*Imaginary Bonnets* 59).

EARTH MAGIC

In the epigraph to her seventh collection, *Geomantic* (2016), Meehan gives us the definition of *geomantic* from the Greek as "Earth divination," "a method of divination that interprets markings on the ground or the patterns formed by tossed handfuls of soil, rocks, or sand" (*Geomantic* back cover). The volume's epigraph, Ciaran Carson's "Indefatigable dazzling / terrestrial strangeness," reinforces the potential for enchantment when confronting a living earth. Meehan suggests in these poems that despite the alienations of modernity, we might remember how to be in dynamic relation with a natural world whose capacity to defamiliarize and dazzle is enduring. In *Geomantic*, earth memory and magic emerge as the very source of poetry, where the moon "rises with the vowels" and the resulting poem is "muse magic wrought from the power of

nine" (43). The poems reverberate with numerological significance: "Count the syllables, a perfect line: / the way moon rises
with the vowels" opens the poem "The Moon Rose Over an Open
Field." Meehan reclaims throughout this volume the mystical
power of the number nine, that symbol of wholeness, completion,
and fullness throughout world mythology, especially in the stories
of the old Norse god Odin, who gained spiritual insight for transformation by drinking the mead of poetry magic.

We might say, then, that *Geomantic* is a vitalist volume by
design with each poem a carefully wrought spell. The repetition
of the number nine, each nine-line poem with nine syllables per
line and the total number of poems divisible by nine, echoes the
earth magic of the book's title. Moreover, Irish mythology incorporates as magical that square root of nine, the number three in
the triple spiral of passage graves, the triple goddess Brigid, the
tricolor flag, the shamrock. Shored up by such muse magic, Meehan
reached through these poems into the otherworld: she took up her
post as Poetry Professor of Ireland shortly after Seamus Heaney's
death, and mindful of his nine-line "Postcard from Iceland,"
her choice of form became both a tribute to him as well as a support to herself, "Seamus's hand that I could grab." Thus, written
while Meehan served as Poetry Professor of Ireland (2013–2015),
Geomantic employs a spare and supple form from both the exi-
gencies of life in a public role and the lived experiences of social
and political struggle, the inner life always informed by soundings
from the outer.

The spell poems in *Geomantic* often create through their
prosody aural layers of rhyme that create and reinforce meaning.
Strikingly, many of the volume's poems employ an abcd/e/abcd
rhyme scheme, an encircling structure that gives special emphasis to the central, unrhymed line. An early poem in the volume
employs this nesting structure ironically: the drowned daughter
in "The Trust" has been abandoned by church, state, and family:
"Our Lady" and "new austerity" open and close the poem with
"daughter" and "water" naming through rhyme the drowning

of the daughter in the Liffey. The unrhymed central line in this poem—"left her to the city's chartered streets"—turns the layers of rhymed lines from the possibility of a protective embrace toward isolation and despair. This poem echoes in a quiet way Meehan's earlier "The Statue of the Virgin at Granard Speaks," where the young Ann Lovett receives no support or protection from communal institutions whose moral charges have been perverted; in the ironically titled "The Trust," Meehan finds the same institutional failures decades on. Another dead child appears at the center of "The Spank," where neither a grandson's inherent gifts nor the status of a "good family" protect the boy from an early death to drug use. In the poem, the grandmother registers bewilderment that class status and personal endowments are not enough: "Good family, everything to live for" floats alone between the rhymed couplets of crown/down, wild/child, bought it/thought it, heart/smart as if to suggest that a family's naïve trust in the status quo has left them unmoored. These poems of witness in *Geomantic* remind us again that Meehan remains faithful to the shamanic charge of her role as a significant voice for her community.

QUILTING *GEOMANTIC*

Earthly and cosmic, personal and communal, multigenerational and transpersonal, the poems in *Geomantic* are also poetry panels in the communal artifact of the quilt. Meehan has drawn for her formal structure on the memorial quilts for the youth lost to drug addiction in Dublin's inner-city communities; an outgrowth of the memorial quilts honoring the memories of those lost to AIDS in the United States, these quilts "caught on in Ireland because so many intravenous drug users got the virus" and died from AIDS:

> Every February 1st, St. Brigid's Day . . . there's a memorial service, cross faith, in what was one of the churches of my childhood, Our Lady of Lourdes, Sean McDermott Street. . . . I always try to attend even if I am not there as 'poet'—I go to remember my own family members & friends & neighbours who died through

addiction. The different family networks (community support groups from all over the island) hang their memorial quilts from the high walls of the church and they are there throughout the service. I think they are the bravest, most powerful, iteration of memory and [they] challenge the official lip service paid to the deceased. (Meehan, personal email, 29 October 2016)

Integrating the visual and symbolic power of these quilts, *Geomantic*'s series of eighty-one nine-line poetry panels form a verbal quilt of memory. The cover design, made from Meehan's own maturing visual art, echoes the volume's structure, with nine squares representing stylized landscapes in vivid rainbow colors, three blocks repeating three times each. Recalling geomancy's cast handful of dirt, this cover also evokes cast runic tiles.

Public memorial in these poems is stitched to private memory through a matriarchal line in "The Quilt," "a simple affair—nine squares / by nine squares . . . my grandmother's quilt I slept under / the long and winding nights of childhood." For Meehan, the quilts embody

the compassion and desperation experienced, especially by the poorer communities, who have, I believe, been abandoned by successive governments in the face of huge crisis, of which addiction is the most harrowing aspect. I felt, in this year of commemoration, 2016, that these quilts would be my inspiration and source, because they mean more to me, and speak more profoundly to me, than many of the 'official' or state commemorative gestures. If measured by the aspirations of the founding principles of the Republic, these communities have been betrayed. (Meehan, personal email, 29 October 2016)

Meehan's poem "The Commemorations Take Our Minds Off the Now" addresses the forgetting of the dire circumstances of the present. Focusing on the past makes possible the power relations for increasingly insane current conditions for the poor: "A boon to

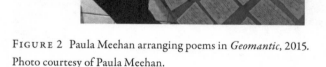

FIGURE 2 Paula Meehan arranging poems in *Geomantic*, 2015.
Photo courtesy of Paula Meehan.

the Government; they rule / in the knowledge that none can keep track." In the face of this erasure of the now, the narrator restores the present: "I commemorate / the poor going round and round the bend. / How mad do you have to be to make / sense of the state of the State we're in?" (*G* 58).

The neoliberal policies that created the financial collapse of 2008 were followed in Ireland and elsewhere by austerity measures, both intentional and de facto, that rewarded elites who continue to plunder both the earth and the populace. The resulting disenfranchisements have created the conditions for dangerous forms of authoritarianism among despairing populations for whom a failure of historical memory could promise social, economic, and ecological catastrophe.

FIGURE 3 *Geomantic* arranged like quilt squares on the kitchen table, 2015. Photo courtesy of Paula Meehan.

THE PUBLIC POEM

With the legacy of Yeats's "Easter 1916" and the increasingly relevant "The Second Coming," Seamus Heaney's "Casualty" and "Punishment," and Eavan Boland's "A Doll's Museum in Dublin," Irish poetry has had neither the luxury nor the inclination to marginalize the poem arising from the public event. Meehan is especially well-equipped to see the ways public events and private lives are mutually informing. In 2015 Meehan was a key figure in organizing the Artist's Campaign to Repeal the Eighth Amendment, a first step toward legalizing abortion in the Republic. That activity and outcome resonate deeply with what may still be the poem for which Meehan is best known. "The Statue of the Virgin at Granard Speaks" was inspired by the tragic story of the young Ann Lovett, who died giving birth outdoors in the winter of 1984 as a result of the antiabortion policies of the Irish State and the Catholic Church, though Meehan did not publish it until half a decade later, in her third collection, *The Man Who Was Marked by Winter* (1991). Andrew Auge has described the poem as "perhaps the most notable public poem in recent Irish literary history" (194), and the Irish public seems to agree: in 2015 the poem was voted among the ten short-listed for RTÉ television's "A Poem for Ireland." Alluding to the 1985 moving statues phenomena, when Catholics across Ireland claimed to have seen apparitions of the moving hands and eyes of statues of the Virgin Mary, Meehan gives voice to the statue of the Virgin in the grotto where Ann Lovett died in childbirth. Here the Virgin emerges as radically attentive to both the pleasures of the body and the cycle of the seasons, with no desire for either the name she has been given or the role she has been assigned: "My being / cries out to be incarnate, incarnate, / maculate and tousled in a honeyed bed" (*MMW* 44). Revealing herself as a thoroughly pagan goddess, the Virgin prays to the sun for release from the guilt she feels over the tragic death of the child she failed to help: "O sun, / center of our foolish dance, / burning heart of stone / molten mother of us all / hear me and have pity" (*MMW* 44). In this poem the life-giving properties of an animate natural world have been subverted by a life-denying religion and "the child / who came with fifteen summers to her name" can find no solace. Meehan animates stone, shape-shifting Mary into a nature goddess of an earth-based religion who would bless rather than demonize female sexuality (Auge 201). The poem does the cultural work of offering a counternarrative to a tragic communal event.

PSYCHIC SKYPE

In *Geomantic,* Meehan explicitly links earthly and cosmic forces, the everyday and the magical. "The Grimoire" literally names a textbook of magic, including spells and divination. But with "you call it my book of shadows" and "I scry," we are invited to read *Geomantic* itself as a grimoire. Enclosed by the first and last line rhymes of shadows/window, the poem paradoxically expands its scope as the lines move inward with the astrological rhyme of stars/ Mars. "The Grimoire" explores the relationship between human agency and "a fated course," as if to acknowledge that the return of power to an animate natural world and cosmos leaves who or what's in charge up for grabs. In this case, the human "us" emerges as "twinned / lost souls" (*G* 20).

In "The Feathers," the narrator playfully undercuts astral flight, first by evoking the shaman's transformation into bird with the poem's title and first line, "To be so far up riding thermals / . . . is to enter the realm of the hawk" (*G* 26), and then by locating the narrator and her companion on "the sad road of the earth-bound" engaged in "crazy talk" (*G* 26). "Thermals" rhymes with both "angel" and "carnal" as all the realms emerge and converge in the poem: May/play/Milky Way. This is the poet of Meehan's "Deadwood" with its playfully ironic rhymes; of the whimsically titled selected poems, *As If By Magic*; of the wry voice in "The Tantric Master" in *Dharmakaya*. Rather than correctives, these poems explore the uncomfortable and uncanny dimensions of embracing a belief in animism and decentering human agency. A modern subject working to retrieve premodern ways of knowing is indeed on a kind of psychic skype along with childhood ghosts and angels. David Abram points at the discomfort: "How do we analyse magical consciousness as part of a wider process of consciousness when our structures of thought have been shaped by a rationalism that does not recognize magical consciousness as a legitimate form of knowledge?" (12–13). Perhaps in some moments, Meehan's narrators can only evoke but not entirely inhabit such a magical state of mind.

OUR OWN BEE-LOUD GLADE

The closing poem of *Geomantic*, "The Island," is set in one of Meehan's spiritual homes on the island of Ikaria in Greece. Her early training as a classicist finds lived expression through her months of embodied writing on that island and communion with its rhythms: "At home again on Ikaria, / our own bee-loud glade" (*G* 95). This opening line of Meehan's final poem in the volume manages to name not only Greece but also Yeats and the Irish literary tradition (especially "The Lake Isle of Innisfree"), as well as the influence of the American Romantic tradition in Yeats's echoing of Henry David Thoreau's *Walden*. And, indeed, each of the poems in this last section of the book participate in such an accordion expansion and contraction, across time and space, across thresholds of life and death, across species, from the earthly to the cosmic.

In these final poems narrator and companions are thoroughly immersed in the nonhuman and more than willing to reframe *being human* within a larger biosphere. "The Food Chain" playfully resists anthropocentrism as the narrator joyfully consumes her environment, both literally and figuratively, even as it consumes her: "I could eat the moon, the breaking waves, / the moonlight sifting through the pine trees; / I could eat you, my beauty" (*G* 91). Her companion's gaze takes in the cat, the cat "stalks the plump frog," the frog the bug, all the while humans eating and being eaten: "we eat little silver fishes / and are nibbled on in turn by flies" (*G* 91). As with the title of each poem in the volume, this one employs "the" as article, definite in its materiality and particularity as if charged, weighted, substantial. Yet there is also the planetary and cosmic as the poem lands with "the shine of this blood moon's rise" (91).

"The Road to Agios Kirikos" follows the narrator and her companion after they have become ghosts with "all / the time in the world," taking in the world at all scales, "the wall / where the glow-worms between the stones / sing the stardust of which they're made" (*G* 92). And the poem following, "The Handful of Earth," continues the insistent linking of near and far, visible and invisible, ordinary and magical: "Under the paths stars make, wild birds call" (*G* 93). Here methods of divination converge: geomancy, tea leaves, *I Ching*, tarot, and more. In anthropologist Susan Greenwood's terms, this is magic as an alternative world-view, the otherworld become ontological reality: "an awareness of the spirituality of the everyday, the earth, the body with all its attendant thoughts, feelings and emotions, and a sense of the interconnectedness of it all. This is magical consciousness, . . . the capability of 're-enchanting the world' for those who experience it" (xi). There is also in these final poems boundary-crossing in abundance as in "The Sea Cave," where sexuality is fluid, quite literally in the water, woman desiring woman, echoing earlier poems in the volume like "The New Regime," in which "[h]er mouth's rimed with my milk" (*G* 78), and "The Withdrawal"'s "I crave her cool comfort, her deep shade" (*G* 79). Earth, water, sky. Bee, hawk, snake, cats, owl: "The Island" is where the narrator is "home" with all of them, the humans and their human categories "unsettled and creaturely" (*G* 95).

INTERVIEW

....

IMPERIAL TRAUMA, WHICH IS WHAT IT WAS, 2019

PAULA MEEHAN: I am researching the fantastic material on the Meehans of Monto, and just recently I found a headline in the *Irish Independent* of 1914 saying that my great-grandfather is arrested by the Dublin Metropolitan Police with his gang, and the headline of the column is "Den of Thieves." He's there in the brothel beside the shop—the shop next door—and the police come. He's been with his gang, which includes this amazing woman (I'll tell you about her in a minute). They've been knocking off depots. Now, depots are where the imported goods are stored when they arrive by sea or train. They're stored in depots or warehouses along the docks, and then they're distributed. So, they're not robbing shops. There's a riot of up to (and this is the cold reporting of the paper) fifty women in the street, obviously resisting the police raid. They attack the police to try to stop them from arresting the gang.

That's put me on a whole new line of inquiry, and the interesting person there is this character I found in the 1911 census. She's nineteen, and her name was Christine Toole. She caught my eye there in my great-grandmother's brothel, because she's entered as speaking both Irish and English. (She's down as a lodger, which is what all the girls were entered as, or servants.) She's one of the rare mentions in that area, the Monto, of an Irish speaker. And the thing about the relationship between the community there and the authority making the census, which of course is the colonial administration, is that nobody told the truth to that power. But I fixed on her because she speaks Irish. What's a nineteen-year-old "servant" or "lodger" doing speaking Irish in the tenements of the red-light district? Okay, so I started on that line of inquiry, and Terry Fagan, the great oral historian of the Monto, says he has a recording of her made when she was a very old woman. She is in my great-grandmother's brothel at nineteen and she's in this gang of robbers at twenty-four, the only woman.

My grandfather always said to me that I took after his mother, Anna, the madame, because she always had her nose in a book. "She was a great reader, my mother," he'd say. In the census, though, she signs, as head of household, with an "X" and in other written records I've come across, there it is—her X. She's not even living with Charles, her husband. Him of the "Den of Thieves" headline. Christine Toole turned out to be an intelligence officer for Michael Collins, in the lead-up to the War of Independence, and her job was to collect information from the girls—the pillow talk. Aldeborough House, the huge barracks for the soldiers, is just down the way at the Five Lamps. So, she was collecting. . . . I love this new material that I'm finding out about her. During the War of Independence she would debrief the girls and get the soldiers' and the dockers' chat and bring it to Phil Shanahan's pub on the corner of Mabbot Street and Montgomery Street. And he'd go there, Michael Collins, to the upstairs room and debrief her and other informants of these crucial bits information to put together a map of troop movements and commanding officers' habits. I'm trying to chase her up, and then it turns out that Anna Meehan, my great-grandmother, her maiden name is Anna Plunkett, from Purdon Street, and they're a family with Republican connections. So here my family history, hard and all as it is to pin down, intersects with those events of the revolutionary era. It is such a complex and multifaceted lens to have on the times. And it has taught me that my natural habitat is in the chasm between the folklore and the written archive. And I am completely at home there!

KATHRYN KIRKPATRICK: Absolutely.

PM: Another interesting thing is James Joyce often named his most pious characters after disreputable streets: Father

Purdon, for example, is named for Purdon Street, which had the densest concentration of women sex workers, the street where my great-grandmother was born and where she married out of at the age of thirteen and a half, already pregnant. Is it any wonder I feel compelled to channel her? I feel very close to her.

The street my grandfather, her son, was born on, Mabbot Street, is now James Joyce Street because that was the entrance to his Nighttown in the Circe episode of *Ulysses*. I like to think he would have seen my beloved grandparents as children about the Monto.

So, I'm chasing many hares and also very aware that the last of the elders are going, and going fast. And Terry Fagan was one of the few links to those memories, but you see, the problem with Terry's archives is he promised these old women, and many of them were old prostitutes, that he wouldn't ever let anyone else hear the tapes. He tells great stories, but there's questions around the reliability of the stories because if the written record is difficult, the oral one is all story and the stories grow tails, and legs and mouth to ear to mouth. . . . Well, that's the folk tradition. So, I don't know what I'm going to do with this material, but it's coming to me sweetly. Not only that, but one of my cousins got in touch to say that her friend is a medium, and there was this stuff coming through from someone called Anna who wants to get in touch with me!

KK: Oh my!

PM: Normally, I go to material or align research with an ask. I'm after something. But with this, I don't know what I'm after.

KK: You're being led.

PM: Well, it feels more like I'm being shown, and it's complex because I'd be very aware that . . . I mean, I've also researched the lives of the prostitutes, you know?

KK: Yes.

PM: That isn't a laughing matter; it's Our Lady of the Apocalypse. It's the end of that economy when the soldiers left. It was really tough, and I just saw the last shimmering and even ghosts of it as a child. Imperial trauma, which is what it was.

AFTERWORD

———

In Elaine Crowley's film about Paula Meehan and her work, *Working with Metal*, Luz Mar Gonzalez Arias says of Meehan's poems: "They have led me. They have accompanied me. They have been my fellow travelers in the process of growing up." Like Gonzalez Arias, my engagement with Meehan's work has had the quality of a rite of passage. Raised by parents who knew quite intimately what it meant to be poor, I lived the aftershocks of their trauma, which on some levels became my own. Meehan has made the interior life of a woman growing up in an inner-city Dublin community matter. In "Imaginary Bonnets with Real Bees in Them," Meehan presents herself as a child insisting on her own lived experience, writing an elegy for her dead dog, Prince, instead of the assigned composition about milk (4). Later, she stands before Sister Philippa to strike back at being frog-marched through the school. It's hard not to feel the truth of this: "Being thrown out of school was the best thing that could have happened to me" (8). Speaking up and speaking back to a class hierarchy that would have silenced her prepared her for making working-class lives visible not only for Irish readers but also for the rest of us.

This book has made the relationship between writer and critic more explicit than most books of criticism usually do. Yet as Meehan herself has observed, revealing the skein of connection between commentator and subject, between poet and critic is apt: "Poems are like mirrors. People look into them and the poem is reading them, their education, their vocabulary, their emotional tenor; it reads what they bring to it" (Allen Randolph, "Conversation"). I have brought a childhood of class trauma to her work and learned that it is not only survivable but also might hold alternative perspectives: a certain distance on the values of an avaricious neoliberal culture, a sure resistance to bourgeois gender roles, an openness to premodern conceptions of a living earth. And as a practicing poet, I embrace the dictum in "Peace": "I might undo the State's betrayal: / redemption through a mastery of form" (*G* 60).

Moreover, Meehan's Poetry Professor of Ireland lectures, as I hope I have demonstrated, offer innovations and interventions in the lyric essay as a form. These lectures are a quiet example of the magical consciousness with which this study of her work lands. Combining associative, intuitive ways of knowing that actively engage with and even take their formal cues from the nonhuman with a more familiar linear and rational way of knowing, Meehan's method informs an approach I have been inspired by her essays to develop. Animal poetics, a way of engaging with poems that represent other animals as much as possible on their own terms, is a project that has emerged alongside the finishing of this book (Kirkpatrick "Doing the Human").

So Paula Meehan continues her work, and I continue mine. And I know our conversations will also continue—always on the page, sometimes online, and, when I'm lucky, in person. Even as I trace here one arc of her writing through *Geomantic*, her new book arrives: *The Solace of Artemis* (2023), a splendid continuation of her work. The volume includes "For the Hungry Ghosts," a series inspired by the Hades episode in Joyce's *Ulysses*. The poems are part of a remarkable public project of performances, *Ulysses 2.2*, that unfolded in 2022, marking the centenary of Joyce's masterwork, when writers, musicians, and artists were commissioned to respond with their own creative new work to an episode in *Ulysses*. Meehan has described the series as addressing the legacy of imperial trauma in her life and lineage, and the voice she brings to this wider arena of poetic investigation draws on archival material of her own family, especially her great-grandmother Anna Plunket, who was one of the last of the Dublin madames. Thus, with the heft of her already substantial oeuvre behind her, these new poems reenter the Irish literary tradition once more with forgotten lives and voices, certain, once again to change the narrative of Irish literary history.

WORKS CITED

———

Abram, David. *The Spell of the Sensuous*. Vintage, 1997.

Adams, Carol J., and Josephine Donovan. *Animals and Women: Feminist Theoretical Explorations*. Duke UP, 1995.

Allen Randolph, Jody. "The Body Politic: A Conversation with Paula Meehan." Paula Meehan, special issue of *An Sionnach,* vol. 5, no. 1&2, spring/fall 2009.

———. *Close to the Next Moment: Interviews from a Changing Ireland*. Carcanet Press Limited, 2010.

———. "A Conversation with Paula Meehan about *Geomantic*." *YouTube*, uploaded by UCD Library Special Collections, 14 June 2016, www.youtube .com/watch?v=iQ7ly8smv9Y.

Allison, Dorothy. "A Cure for Bitterness." *Critical Trauma Studies: Understanding Violence, Conflict, and Memory in Everyday Life*, edited by Monica J. Casper and Eric Wertheimer, New York University Press, 2016, pp. 244–255.

Auge, Andrew. *A Chastened Communion: Modern Irish Poetry and Catholicism*. Syracuse UP, 2013.

Baker, Steve. *Postmodern Animal*. Reaktion Books, 2000.

Banerjee, Subhankar, and Matthiessen, Peter. Arctic National Wildlife Refuge: Seasons of Life and Land: a Photographic Journey. Mountaineers Books, 2003.

Barlett, Peggy. "Reason and Re-enchantment in Cultural Change: Sustainability in Higher Education." *Current Anthropology,* vol. 49, 2008, pp. 1077–98.

Bowker, John. "Buddhism." *Oxford Dictionary of World Religions*. Ed. John Bowker, Oxford University Press, 1997, 974.

Boyle, Mark. "Cleaning Up After the Celtic Tiger: Scalar 'Fixes' in the Political Ecology of Tiger Economics." *Transactions of the Institute of British Geographers*, vol. 27, no. 2, 2002, pp. 173–90.

Bowker, John. *The Oxford Dictionary of World Religions*. United Kingdom, Oxford University Press, 1999.

Brandes, Rand. "Mercury in Taurus: W.B. Yeats and Ted Hughes." *South Carolina Review,* vol. 43, no. 1, 2010, pp. 198–210.

Brown, Laura. "Not Outside the Range: One Feminist Perspective on Psychic Trauma." *Trauma: Explorations in Memory*, edited by Cathy Caruth, Johns Hopkins UP, 1995.

Butler, Alison. *Victorian Occultism and the Making of Modern Magic: Invoking Tradition*. Palgrave MacMillan, 2011.

Butler, Judith. *Precarious Life: The Powers of Mourning and Violence*. Verso, 2004.

Caruth, Cathy. *Unclaimed Experience: Trauma, Narrative, and History*. Johns Hopkins UP, 1996.

Chakrabarty, Dipesh. "Climate and Capital: On Conjoined Histories." *Critical Inquiry*, vol. 42, no. 1, 2014, pp. 1–23.

Combat Poverty Agency. "Richer but More Unequal: the distribution of income in Ireland. Poverty Briefings 11. Combat Poverty Publications. www.lenus.ie/handle/10147/136803

Cronin, Michael. "Ireland's Disappeared: Suicide, Violence, and Austerity." *Ireland Under Austerity: Neoliberal Crisis, Neoliberal Solutions,* edited by Colin Coulter and Angela Nagel, Manchester UP, 2015, pp. 133–50.

Crowley, Elaine. *Working with Metal*. *Vimeo*, uploaded 10 November 2009, https://vimeo.com/7536129.

Deckard, Sharae. "Introduction: Reading Ireland's Food, Energy, and Climate." Food, Energy, Climate: Irish Culture and World-Ecology, special issue of *Irish University Review*, vol. 49, no. 1, 2019.

Dickie, Gloria. "Most Polar Bears to Disappear by 2100, Study Predicts." *The Guardian*, 20 July 2020, www.theguardian.com/environment/2020/jul/20/most-polar-bears-to-disappear-by-2100-study-predicts-aoe.

Dorgan, Theo. "An Interview with Paula Meehan." *Colby Quarterly,* vol. 28, 1992, pp. 265–69.

Eliade, Mircea. *Shamanism: Archaic Techniques of Ecstasy*. 1951. Princeton UP, 2020.

Elias, Amy J., and Christian Moraru. *The Planetary Turn: Relationality and Geoaesthetics in the Twenty-First Century*. Northwestern UP, 2015.

"Enrapture" V. Oxford English Dictionary, Oxford UP, July 2023, https://doi.org/10.1093/OED/6109307358.

Evernden, Neil. "Beyond Ecology: Self, Place, and the Pathetic Fallacy." *The Ecocritical Reader: Landmarks in Literary Ecology*, edited by Cheryll Glotfelty and Harold Fromm, U of Georgia P, 1996, pp. 92–104.

Falci, Eric. "Meehan's Stanzas and the Irish Lyric After Yeats." *An Sionnach: A Journal of Literature, Culture, and the Arts*, vol. 5 no. 1, 2009, p. 226–238.

Farrier, David. *Anthropocene Poetics: Deep Time, Sacrifice Zones, and Extinction*. U of Minnesota P, 2019.

Fears, Darryl. "As Ice Melts, Polar Bears Migrate North." *Washington Post*, 7 January 2015, www.washingtonpost.com/news/speaking-of-science/wp/2015/01/07/as-ice-melts-polar-bears-migrate-north.

Federici, Silvia. *Caliban and the Witch*. Autonomedia, 2004.

———. *Re-enchanting the World: Feminism and the Politics of the Commons*. PM Press, 2019.

Felstiner, John. *Can Poetry Save the Earth?* Yale UP, 2009.

Fenster, Tovi. "Gender and the City: The Different Formations of Belonging." *A Companion to Feminist Geography*. Blackwell, 2005.

Foley, Daniel. "Foreword." *Irish Gardens*. Edward Hyams and William MacQuitty. Macmillan, 1967, pp. 1–8.

Frazer, James. *The Golden Bough*. 1922. MacMillan, 1951.

Gaard, Greta. *Critical Ecofeminism*. Lexington Books, 2017.

Ghosh, Amitav. *The Nutmeg's Curse: Parables for a Planet in Crisis*. U of Chicago P, 2021.

Gibson-Graham, J. K. Stephen Resnick, and Richard Wolff. "Class in a Poststructuralism Frame." *Class and Its Others*, edited by J. K. Gibson-Graham, Stephen Resnick, and Richard Wolff, U of Minnesota P, 2000.

Giesler, Patric V. "Magic, Witchcraft and the Otherworld." *American Ethnologist*, vol. 29, no. 1, 2002.

Green, Miranda and Stephen Green. *The Quest of the Shaman: Shape-Shifters, Sorcerers, and Spirit Healers of Ancient Europe.* Thames & Hudson, 2005.

Greenwood, Susan. *The Anthropology of Magic.* Routledge, 2009.

Grene, Nicholas. "Introduction." Paula Meehan's Poetry Professor of Ireland Lecture, "The Solace of Artemis." Trinity College Dublin, November 2014. https://www.tcd.ie/English/literary-arts/Podcasts.php.

Hall, Stuart. "The Meaning of New Times." *Stuart Hall: Critical Dialogues in Cultural Studies*, edited by David Morley and Kuan-Hsing Chen, Routledge, 1996, pp. 223–37.

———. "On Postmodernism and Articulation: An Interview with Stuart Hall." *Stuart Hall: Critical Dialogues in Cultural Studies*, edited by David Morley and Kuan-Hsing Chen, Routledge, 1996, pp. 131–50.

Haraway, Donna. *When Species Meet.* U of Minnesota P, 2007.

Hayden, Joanne. "I Believe that Two Lines of Poetry Can Save a Life." *The Independent.ie*, 6 May 2018, www.independent.ie/entertainment/theatre-arts/i-believe-that-two-lines-of-poetry-can-save-a-life-paula-meehan-36865589.html.

Heaney, Seamus. The Redress of Poetry. Faber &Faber, 1995.

Howard, Ben. "'Why Did the Buddhadharma Come to Ireland?': Buddhist Themes in Recent Irish Poetry." *An Sionnach,* vol. 1, no. 2, 2005, pp. 65–75.

Huggan, Graham, and Helen Tiffin. *Postcolonial Ecocriticism: Literature, Animals, Environment.* Routledge, 2010.

Jex, Catherine. "Grizzly Polar Bear Hybrids Spotted in Canadian Arctic." *Science Nordic,* 6 June 2016, www.sciencenordic.com/denmark-evolution-greenland-science-special/grizzly-polar-bear-hybrids-spotted-in-canadian-arctic/1434185.

Keohane, Kieran, and Kuhling, Carmen. The Domestic, Moral and Political Economies of Post-Celtic Tiger Ireland: What Rough Beast? Manchester University Press, 2015.

Kirkpatrick, Kathryn. "Doing the Human Differently: Rabbits and Hares in Contemporary Irish Poetry." *Contemporary Irish Poetry and the Climate Crisis*, edited by Andrew J. Auge and Eugene O'Brien, Routledge, 2022, pp. 74–94.

———. *Our Held Animal Breath: Poems.* WordTech Editions, 2012.

———. *The Fisher Queen: New & Selected Poems.* Salmon Press, 2019.

LaDuke, Winona. *All Our Relations*. South End Press, 1999.

Lamb, Keith, and Patrick Bowe. *A History of Gardening in Ireland*. National Botanic Gardens, 1995.

Lepselter, Susan. *The Resonance of Unseen Things*. U of Michigan P, 2016.

Linebaugh, Peter. "Foreword." *Re-enchanting the World: Feminism and the Politics of the Commons,* by Silvia Federici, PM Press, 2019.

McGovern, Iggy. *20/12: Twenty Irish Poets Respond to Science in Twelve Lines*. Dedalus Press, 2012.

Meehan, Paula. *Cell*. New Island Books, 2000.

———. *As If By Magic: Selected Poems*. Dedalus Press, 2020.

———. *Dharmakaya*. Carcanet Press, 2000.

———. *Geomantic*. Dedalus Press, 2019.

———. "The Hermit's Hut." *Sources: Letters from Irish People on Sustenance for the Soul,* edited by Marie Heaney, Town Hall, 1999.

———. *Imaginary Bonnets with Real Bees in Them (The Poet's Chair: Writings from the Ireland Chair of Poetry)*. University College Dublin Press, 2016.

———. *The Man Who Was Marked By Winter*. Gallery Press, 1991.

———. *Mysteries of the Home*. Bloodaxe Books, 1996. Rpt. Dedalus Press, 2013.

———. *Painting Rain*. Carcanet Press, 2009.

———. *Pillow Talk*. Gallery Press, 1994.

——— *Reading the Sky*. Beaver Row Press, 1986.

———. *Return and No Blame*. Beaver Row Press, 1984.

———. "The Solace of Artemis." *20/12: Twenty Irish Poets Respond to Science in Twelve Lines*, edited by Iggy McGovern, Dedalus Press, 2012.

———. *The Solace of Artemis*. Dedalus Press, 2023.

Merchant, Carolyn. *The Columbia Guide to American Environmental History*. Columbia UP, 2002.

———. *The Death of Nature*. HarperCollins, 1980.

———. *Reinventing Eden: The Fate of Nature in Western Culture*. Routledge, 2004.

Mies, Maria, and Vandana Shiva. *Ecofeminism*. Zed Books, 1993.

Mortuza, Shamasad. *The Figure of the Shaman in Contemporary British Poetry*. Cambridge Scholars, 2013.

Nixon, Rob. *Slow Violence and the Environmentalism of the Poor*. Harvard UP, 2011.

O'Halloran, Eileen, and Kelli Maloy. "An Interview with Paula Meehan." *Contemporary Literature,* vol. 43, no. 1, 2002, 1–27.

Oliver, Mary. *A Poetry Handbook.* Ecco, 1994.

Ortner, Sherry. *Making Gender: The Politics and Erotics of Culture.* Beacon, 1996.

Parmigiani, Giovanna. "Exploring Magical Consciousness as a Form of Knowledge: A Conversation with Susan Greenwood." *YouTube,* uploaded by Harvard Divinity School, 18 October 2021, www.youtube.com/watch ?v=NtE3yHDqfpY.

"Planet, N." *Oxford English Dictionary,* Oxford UP, March 2024, https://doi .org/10.1093/OED/1173352017.

Plumwood, Val. *Feminism and the Mastery of Nature.* Routledge,1993.

———. "Nature in the Active Voice." *Climate Change and Philosophy,* edited by Ruth Irwin, Continuum, 2010, pp. 32–47.

Praga, Inéz. "Interview with Paula Meehan." *Ireland in Writing: Interviews with Writers and Academics,* edited by Jaqueline Hurtley et al., Rodopi, 1998.

Press Association. "Polar Bear Ancestors Came from Ireland." *The Guardian,* 7 July 2011, www.theguardian.com/science/2011/jul/07/polar-bear -ancestors-ireland.

Reed, T.V. "Toward an Environmental Justice Ecocriticism." *The Environmental Justice Reader,* edited by J. Adamson, M. Evans, R. Stein, University of Arizona Press, 2002.

Roediger, David. "'More Than Two Things': The State of the Art of Labor History." *New Working-Class Studies,* edited by John Russo and Sherry Lee Linkon, Cornell UP, 2005, pp. 32–41.

Russell, Jeffrey Burton. "Witch Hunt." Britannica Academic, 2023. https:// academic-eb-com.proxy006.nclive.org/levels/collegiate/article/witch-hunt /637728. Accessed 8 Sept. 2024.

Scheese, Don. "Desert Solitaire: Counter-Friction to the Machine in the Garden." *The Ecocriticism Reader: Landmarks in Literary Ecology,* edited by Cheryll Glotfelty and Harold Fromm, U of Georgia P, 1996, pp. 303–21.

Seager, Jonim and Mona Domosh. *Putting Women in Place: Feminist Geographers Make Sense of the World.* Guilford Press, 2001.

Sered, Danielle. Untranscribed interview with Paula Meehan. Special Collections Archives. Woodruff Library, Emory University, Atlanta, GA, 1999.

Shiva, Vandana. *Biopiracy: The Plunder of Nature and Knowledge*. South End Press, 1997.

———. *Earth Democracy: Justice, Sustainability, and Peace*. South End Press, 2005.

Sivaraksa, Sulak. "Economic Aspects of Social and Environmental Violence from a Buddhist Perspective." *Buddhist-Christian Studies,* vol. 22, 2002, pp. 47–60.

Snyder, Gary. B.A. thesis, "The Dimensions of a Haida Myth." Reed College of Portland, Oregon, 1951; Rpt. "He Who Hunted Birds in His Father's Village: The Dimensions of a Haida Myth." Counterpoint Press, 2007.

———. *Myths and Texts.* New Directions, 1978.

———. *The Real Work: Interviews and Talks, 1964–1979.* New Directions, 1980.

———. *Regarding Wave.* New Directions, 1970.

———. *Turtle Island.* New Directions, 1974.

Soto-Crespo, Ramóne. "Death and the Diaspora Writer: Hybridity and Mourning in the Work of Jamaica Kincaid." *Contemporary Literature,* vol. 43, no. 2, 2002.

Sperry, Amanda. "Hearth Lessons: Paula Meehan's Ecofeminist Economics." *Études Irlandaises,* vol. 40, no. 2, 2015, pp. 109–20.

———. "An Interview with Paula Meehan." Wake Forest University Press, November 2008, www.wfu.edu/wfupress/An-interview-with-Paula -Meehan.

Spillane, Alison. "The Impact of the Crisis on Irish Women." *Ireland Under Austerity: Neoliberal Crisis, Neoliberal Solutions,* edited by Colin Coulter and Angela Nagel, Manchester UP, 2015, pp. 151–70.

Spivak, Gayatri Chakravorty, and Ellen Rooney. "In a Word. Interview." *Contemporary Literary Criticism*, edited by Jeffrey W. Hunter, vol. 233, Gale, 2007. *Gale Literature Criticism*, link-gale com.proxy006.nclive.org/apps /doc/MXOPMU930217149/LCO? Accessed 7 Sept. 2024. Originally published in *The Essential Difference*, edited by Naomi Schor and Elizabeth Weed, Indiana University Press, 1994, pp. 151–184.

Spivak, Gayatri Chakravorty. *Death of a Discipline*. Columbia UP, 2003.

Steele, Cassie Premo. *We Heal from Memory: Sexton, Lorde, Anzaldúa and the Poetry of Witness*. Palgrave, 2000.

Stevens, Maurice E. "Trauma Is as Trauma Does: The Politics of Affect in Catastrophic Times." *Critical Trauma Studies: Understanding Violence, Conflict, and Memory in Everyday Life.*, edited by Monica J. Casper and Eric Wertheimer, New York University Press, 2016, pp. 19–36.

Thuman, Robert A. F., translator. *The Tibetan Book of the Dead.* Bantam, 1998.

Tillinghast, Richard. *Finding Ireland: A Poet's Explorations of Irish Life and Culture.* U of Notre Dame P, 2008.

Thomsen, Mads Rosendahl. *Mapping World Literature: International Canonization and Transnational Literatures.* Bloomsbury Academic, 2008.

Tong, Rosemarie. *Feminist Thought.* Westview Press, 1998.

Tsing, Anna Lowenhaupt. *The Mushroom at the End of the World: On the Possibility of Life in Capitalist Ruins.* Princeton UP, 2015.

Turner, Victor. *The Forest of Symbols.* Cornell UP, 1967.

Villar-Argáiz, Pilar. "'Act Locally, Think Globally': Paula Meehan's Local Commitment and Global Consciousness." *An Sionnach: A Review of Literature and Culture and the Arts*, vol. 5, no. 1/2, 2009, pp. 180–93.

Vogelsang, E. W. "The Confrontation Between Lilith and Adam: The Fifth Round." *Journal of Analytical Psychology*, vol. 30, no. 2, 1985, pp. 149–63.

Waldau, Paul. *Animal Studies, An Introduction.* Oxford UP, 2013.

Warren, Karen. *Ecofeminist Philosophy: The Western Perspective on What it is and Why it Matters.* Rowan & Littlefield, 2000.

White, Lynn, Jr. "The Historical Roots of Our Ecological Crisis." *The Ecocriticism Reader: Landmarks in Literary Ecology*, edited by Cheryll Glotfelty and Harold Fromm, U of Georgia P, 1996.

Wiig, O., et al. "Polar Bear" IUCN Red List of Threatened Species, https://www.iucnredlist.org/species/22823/14871490. Accessed 7 Sept 2024.

Williams, Raymond. *The Country and the City.* Oxford UP, 1975.

———. *Keywords: A Vocabulary of Culture and Society.* Oxford UP, 1983.

———. *Marxism and Literature.* Oxford UP, 1977.

"World, N." *Oxford English Dictionary*, Oxford UP, June 2024, https://doi.org/10.1093/OED/1495025216.

Yeats, William Butler. "Easter 1916." The Poetry Foundation, https://www.poetryfoundation.org/poems/43289/easter-1916. Accessed 7 Sept 2024.

INDEX

Abbey, Edward, 60
Abram, David, 150, 163
academic writing, poetry and, 12–15
Adams, Carol J., 57–59
AIDS. *See* quilt, imagery
Akhmatova, Anna, 28
allegory, "She-Who-Walks-Among-
   The-People," 20–24
Allison, Dorothy, 27
Amergin, poet, 151–53
American Romanticism, 163
Angus Og, figure, 134
Animals and Women (Adams),
   57–59
animals, reading
   accompaniment, 42
   bears, 120–25
   bees, 115–17
Animal Studies, An Introduction
   (Waldau), 115
animism
   basic perception of, 75
   ecofeminist poetics and, 55–60
   strategic animism, 76–77
   and trees, 77–78
animistic vision,
   and border-crossing sensibility, 72
   in "A Change of Life" sequence in
      Painting Rain, 78–84
   in connection with ecopolitics,
      75–77
   in *The Golden Bough,* 77–78
   in work of Gary Snyder, 73–75

Anzaldúa, Gloria, 25
"Apprentice, The" *(Return and No
   Blame),* 23, 53–54
Arctic National Wildlife Refuge
   Coastal Plain, 120–21
Arias, Luz Mar Gonzalez, 169
ars poetica,
   class trauma and, 35–37
   phrase, 45
art, between science and, 119
Artist's Campaign to Repeal the
   Eighth Amendment, 161
As If By Magic (Meehan), 143–44
Auge, Andrew, 161

Baker, Steve, 119
Banerje, Subhankar, 120–21
Barlett, Peggy, 8
bears, reading, 120–25
bee-loud glade, 163–64
bees, reading, 115–17
being human, reframing, 163–64
"Berlin Diary, 1991" *(Pillow Talk),*
   101
Bishop, Elizabeth, 134, 154
Blake, William, 145
Boland, Eavan, 161
boundary-crossing, 163–64
Bowe, Patrick, 90–91
Boyle, Mark, 49–50
Bronze Age, 64
Brown, Laura, 25–26
Buddhism, 28–30

Butler, Alison, 145
Butler, Judith, 26–27
"Buying Winkles" *(Man Who Was Marked By Winter, The)*, 61–62

Can Poetry Save the Earth? (Felstiner), 7–8
Carson, Ciaran, 155
Cartledge, Paul, 86–87
Caruth, Cathy, 27
Casanova, Pascale, 130–31
Cell (Meehan), 47–48
Celtic Tiger, 147–49. *See also* "Scrying" *(Painting Rain)*
Central Model Girls' School, 16–19
Chakrabarty, Dipesh, 132
"Change of Life, A" *(Painting Rain)*
    conclusion of, 84
    dying chestnut grove in, 81–82
    epigraph of, 78–80
    fifth section of, 82–83
    immersion in demonic aspects of culture, 82
    as poem of major transformation, 80–81
    specter of disorderly women in, 147–48
    taking up Snyder injunctions, 80
"Chapman Lake: Still Life with Bomber" *(Reading the Sky)*, 74–75
"Child's Map of Dublin, A" *(Pillow Talk)*, 63–64
city-country binary, 63–64
Clancy, Juliet, 140–42
class trauma, witnessing
    Buddhist perspective, 28–30
    lack of sacredness, 38–42
    poetry depicting, 30–35
    recording damage done, 35–37
    recovering grievable lives, 24–27
    in "She-Who-Walks-Among-The-People," 20–24

class, term, 36–37
"Cleaning Up after the Celtic Tiger" (Boyle), 49–50
Climate and Capital: On Conjoined Histories" (Chakrabarty), 132
climate change. *See* bears, reading
Close to the Next Moment, 151–52
Coetzee, J. M., 14
Colby Quarterly, 21
colonial gardens, 90–93
Combat Poverty, 48
"Commemorations Take Our Minds Off, The" *(Geomantic)*, 158–59
community experience, archivist of, 43
Condition of the Working Class in England, The (Engels), 10
Contemporary Literature, 50–51
counter-canon, 131
Country and the City, The (Williams), 8
Critical Ecofeminism, 119
Cronin, Michael, 49
Current Biology, 122

Damrosch, David, 130–31
"Deadwood" *(Painting Rain),* 107–8
"Death of a Field" (Meehan), 4
death, meeting, 30–35
Deckard, Sharae, 4
Delo (character). See *Cell* (Meehan)
dependency, interspecies, 114–17
Dharmakaya *(Meehan),* 1, 4, 10–11, 67, 116
    Buddhist perspective in, 27
    echoes of garden trope in, 105–7
    framing of suffering in, 23–24
    and hybrid narratives, 68–71
    language as oppositional discourse in, 35–37
    opening poem of collection, 30–35
    penultimate poem in, 39–41

sacredness in, 38–42
structure of, 25
"Dharmakaya" *(Dharmakaya),* 30–35. See also *Dharmakaya (Meehan)*
"Different Eden, A" *(Pillow Talk),* 101, 106–7
different Eden, finding
  abandoning garden in all conventional forms, 99–108
  cultivated garden as failed domesticity, 97–99
  in "Southside Party" *(Return and No Blame),* 93–94
  in *Reading the Sky,* 94–97
Doll's Museum in Dublin, The" (Boland), 161
domesticity, failure of, 95–97
Domosh, Mona, 60
Donovan, Josephine, 57–59
Dylan, Bob, 29

Eagleton, Terry, 9
earth magic, 155–57
"Easter 1916" (Yeats), 161
"Echoes" *(Return and No Blame),* 54
ecocriticism, 4–5
ecofeminist poetics
  critical ecofeminist poetics of Meehan, 67–68
  definition of, 50–52
  "Instructions to an Absent Husband" as, 55–60
Economic Aspects of Social and Environmental Violence from a Buddhist Perspective" (Hall), 29–30
economy, context, 47–50
Eden, garden, 89
  echo of, 107–8
  See also different Eden, finding
Eliade, Mircea, 152
Elias, Amy, 132

emigration, "Hunger Strike" framing, 95
Engels, Friedrich, 10
environmental injustice, resisting
  ecofeminist poetics, 50–52
  economic contexts, 47–50
  hybrid narratives, 68–71
  "Instructions to an Absent Husband" as ecofeminist poetics, 55–60
  outside/inside dichotomy, 53–55
  poet as shape-shifter, 64–68
  reclaiming street, 60–64
ethnopoetics, 153
European Science Open Forum, 119
Eve (figure). See *Pillow Talk* (Meehan): rereading Christian garden story as myth of origins
Evernden, Neil, 59–60
"Evidence of Tree Worship in the Botanic Gardens" (photograph), 4
"Exact Moment I Became a Poet, The" (Meehan), 15–16, 35–37, 41–42, 44

Falci, Eric, 23
Fall, Christian doctrine of, 89
Falling Sky, The (Kopenawa), 150
Farrier, David, 122
"Feathers, The" *(Geomantic),* 162–63
Federici, Silvia, 8, 147–49
Felstiner, John, 7–8
Fenster, Tovi, 61–62
Finding Ireland (Tillinghast), 91
"First Mammogram" (Kirkpatrick), 69–71
"Fist" *(Dharmakaya),* 33–34, 69
Foley, David, 91
"Food Chain, The" *(Geomantic),* 163–64

Foran, Kay, 15–16. *See also* "Exact Moment I Became a Poet, The" (Meehan)
Forbes Rich List, 48
Frazer, James, 77–78
freedom, redefinition of, 51–52

Gaard, Greta, 119
"Garden of the Sleeping Poet, The" *(Reading the Sky)*, 94–95
garden, term, 94–97
gardenesque, term, 90
gardens
    abandoning in all conventional forms, 99–108
    colonial gardens, 90–93
    cultivated garden as failed domesticity, 97–99
    discussing representation of, 88–90
    echoes of, 105–8
    finding different Eden, 93–108
    objecting to garden as remedy for fallen world, 92–93
gender relations, evocation of. *See* "She-Who-Walks-Among-The-People" *(Pillow Talk)*; women
Geomantic (Meehan), 2–3, 11
    earth magic in, 155–57
    psychic skyping in, 162–63
    quilting, 157–60
    reframing being human in, 163–64
geomantic, term, 155–57
Ghosh, Amitav, 155
    on witch as figure, 145–46
    reframing of writer's role, 150–51
Gibson-Graham, J. K., 9
Golden Bough, The (Frazer), 77–78
Golden Dawn, 145–46
Granny (character). *See* "She-Who-Walks-Among-The-People" *(Pillow Talk)*

Green, Miranda and Stephen, 65–66
Greenwood, Susan, 149–51, 164
Grene, Nicholas, 9, 128
grievable lives, recovering, 24–27
"Grimoire, The" *(Geomantic)*, 162

Haida Indians, 64
Hall, Stuart, 9, 21, 29–30
Harnett, Michael, 66
"He Who Hunted Birds in His Father's Village" (Snyder), 13–14
Heaney, Seamus, 2–3, 156
"Hermit's Hut, The," 92–93
Historical Roots of Our Ecological Crisis, The" (White), 105
History of Gardening in Ireland, A (Lamb), 90–91
"Howth Head" (2014) (interview), 137–42
Huggan, Graham, 5
Hughes, Ted, 143, 152
human exceptionalism
    between science and art, 119
    connections between myth, ritual, and poetry, 125–26
    interspecies dependencies, 114–17
    planetary poetics, 131–36
    quilting *Geomantic,* 157–60
    reading bears, 120–25
    reading bees, 115–17
    river metaphors, 128–30
    wedding of *mythos* and *technos,* 126–28
    "world" as term used in poetry, 130–31
"Hunger Strike" *(Reading the Sky)*, 95–97
husband, term, 100. See also women: and depiction of gardens in *Pillow Talk*
Hyams, Edward, 91
hybrid narratives, 1–14, 68–71, 169–71

"I," confident agency of, 7

Imaginary Bonnets (Meehan). *See*
    "Solace of Artemis, The"
    (Imaginary Bonnets)

"Imaginary Bonnets with Real Bees
    in Them" (*Imaginary Bonnets*),
    114, 117–19, 127–28, 169

IMF-ECB-EU. *See* International
    Monetary Fund–European
    Central Bank–European Union

Imperial Trauma, Which is What it
    is" (2019), 165–68

inside/outside dichotomy, 53–55

"Instructions to an Absent
    Husband" *(Reading the Sky),*
    55–60, 134

International Monetary
    Fund–European Central
    Bank–European Union (IMF-
    ECB-EU), 48–49

interspecies dependency, 114–17

interviews
    "Howth Head" (2014), 137–42
    "Imperial Trauma, Which is
        What it is" (2019), 165–68
    "Inside the Mask is a Human
        Face" (2019), 43–46
    "Life Isn't Going to Be the Same"
        (2020), 85–87
    "Relishing the Conversation"
        (2020), 109–13
    "Self on the Line, The" (2019),
        12–19

Ireland, 8, 105, 131, 147, 161
    AIDS quilts in, 157–60
    colonial gardens, 90–93
    colonial history looming large in
        Reading the Sky, 95–97
    economic boom in, 49–51
    and financial collapse of 2008,
        48–49, 159
    first written mention of poet in,
        151–52

New Ireland, 48, 81
    new poetry in, 128–30
    preconquest-era women in, 103
    public poem in, 161–62
    self-definition within, 35–37
    shamanism in, 151–54
    supporting web of life in, 4–5

"Ireland's Disappeared: Suicide, Vio-
    lence and Austerity" (Cronin),
    49

Irish Gardens (Hyams), 91

Irish Independent, 165

"Is Female to Male as Nature Is to
    Culture?" (Ortner), 58–59

"Island Burial" *(Pillow Talk),* 65

"Island, The" *(Geomantic),* 163

"It Is All I Ever Wanted"
    (Dharmakaya), 39–41

Johnson, Ben, 8

Jordan, June, 5

"Journey to My Sister's Kitchen"
    (Return and No Blame), 54–55

Joyce, James, 166–67

Keohane, Kieran, 48

Kew Gardens, London, 90

Keywords (Williams), 25

Kincaid, Jamaica, 5, 89–90

Kirkpatrick, Kathryn
    "Howth Head" (2014), 137–42
    "Imperial Trauma, Which is
        What it is" (2019), 165–68
    "Inside the Mask is a Human
        Face" (2019), 43–46
    "Life Isn't Going to Be the Same"
        (2020), 85–87
    "Relishing the Conversation"
        (2020), 109–13
    "Self on the Line, The" (2019),
        12–19

Kopenawa, Davi, 150

Kuhling, Carmen, 48

LaDuke, Winona, 73
Lamb, Keith, 90–91
Lepselter, Susan, 5–6
Lhuyd, Edward, 90–91
life in balance. *See* hybrid narratives
Lilith, echo of, 106–7. See also *Pillow Talk* (Meehan): rereading Christian garden story as myth of origins
Linnaeus, Carl, 90
Linebaugh, Peter, 7
"Literacy Class, South Inner City" *(Dharmakaya),* 37, 105–6
literary critics, understanding, 2–3
lives, grievability of, 24–27
"Logging" (Myths and Texts), 73
Lorde, Audre, 25
Lovett, Ann, 161–62

magical state of mind, 149–51
Maloy, Kelli, 50–51
Man Who Was Marked By Winter, The (Meehan), 61–62, 97–99, 161–62
Marx, Karl, 2
Marxism and Literature (Williams), 9
McGahern, John, 139
McGinty, Thom. *See* "Dharmakaya" *(Dharmakaya)*
McGovern, Iggy, 119
Meehan, Paula, 169–71
　allegory in poetry of, 20–24
　between science and art, 119
　synesthesia and, 154–55
　and Buddhism, 28–30
　connecting work with powerful ecopolitics, 75–77
　critical ecofeminist poetics of, 67–68
　as cultural worker, 21–22
　earth magic of, 155–57
　ecocriticism of, 4–5
　employing river metaphor to describe work of, 128–30
　finding different Eden, 93–108
　first appearance of garden in poems of, 93–108
　going beyond human exceptionalism, 114–36
　"Howth Head" (2014), 137–42
　and hybrid narratives, 1–14, 68–71, 169–71
　imagery of quilt in work of, 157–60
　"Imperial Trauma, Which is What it is" (2019), 165–68
　"Inside the Mask is a Human Face" (2019), 43–46
　introduction to works of, 1–2
　"Life Isn't Going to Be the Same" (2020), 85–87
　moving toward animistic vision, 72–84
　objecting to garden as remedy for fallen world, 92–93
　observing first written mention of poet in Ireland, 151–52
　planetary consciousness of, 131–32
　and planetary poetics, 131–36
　and poet as shape-shifter, 64–68
　psychic skype of, 162–63
　and public poem, 161–62
　quilting *Geomantic,* 157–60
　reading "What You Should Know to Be a Poet," 78–84
　reading bears, 120–25
　reading bees, 117–19
　recording richness of vanished childhood community, 51–52
　recovering images of class violence, 26–27
　reframing being human, 163–64

"Relishing the Conversation" (2020), 109–13
resisting environmental injustice, 47–71
restoring garden, 88–108
and self on the line, 12–19
and shamanic poet, 143–64
shamanism and, 151–54
specter of disorderly women in poems of, 147–48
strategic animism of, 76–77
taking up struggle for self-definition, 35–37
Trinity lecture of, 125–26
understanding literary critics, 2–3
wedding of *mythos* and *technos*, 126–28
witnessing class trauma, 20–42
working-class subject matter in works of, 7–9
Merchant, Carolyn, 50, 79, 89, 144
Mies, Maria, 51
Miss Shannon, teacher, 16–19
"Mistle Thrush" *(Dharmakaya)*, 39
modernity
legacies of, 43–44
repressed other of, 144–46
Moraru, Christian, 132
Moretti, Franco, 130–31
Mortuza, Shamasad, 153–54
Mount Stewart, 91
"My Father's Hands That Winter" *(Dharmakaya)*, 34–35
"My Father Perceived as a Vision of St. Francis" *(Pillow Talk)*, 62, 104–5
Mysteries of the Home (Meehan), 23
mythos, wedding of *technos* and, 126–28
myths, 64, 66, 122, 123, 125
Myths and Texts (Snyder), 73–75

"myths are true." *See* Meehan, Paula: Trinity lecture of

nature
holding improper views of. *See* witch, figure
reframing of exploitation of, 52. *See also* ecofeminist politics
Neoplatonic magic, 144–46
"New Regime, The" *(Geomantic)*, 164
"Night Walk" *(Pillow Tak)*, 62
Nixon, Rob, 5
"Not alone the rue in my herb garden" *(Pillow Talk)*, 99–100
Not Outside the Range" (Brown), 25–26

O'Halloran, Eileen, 50–51
Oliver, Mary, 123
"On Being Taken for a Turkish Woman" *(Pillow Talk)*, 62–63
"One Evening in May" *(Pillow Talk)*, 6–7
oppression, evocation of. *See* "She-Who-Walks-Among-The-People" *(Pillow Talk)*
ornamentation, vulnerability to, 15
Ortner, Sherry, 58–59
Others, 50–52, 57–59, 73
Our Held Animal Breath, 43
outside/inside dichotomy, 53–55

Painting Rain (Meehan), 11, 72, 78, 129, 147
finding different Eden in, 107–8
mourning nature in, 84
specter of disorderly women in, 147–48
"Pattern, The" *(Man Who Was Marked by Winter, The)*, 108
patterning, impulse and, 109–13

"Peace" *(Geomantic),* 170
Phoenix Park, horticulture of, 108
Pillow Talk (Meehan), 6–7
  abandoning garden in all conventional forms in, 99–108
  acknowledging potential danger of street, 62–64
  animate nonhuman world in, 115–16
  echoes of garden in collections beyond, 105–8
  opening poem of, 62, 104–5
  owning gendered implications of garden in, 101
  reemergence of colonial dimension of the garden trope, 101
  rereading Christian garden story as myth of origins, 101–3
  revisiting domestic enclosure in, 99–101
"Planet Water" (Meehan), 129–30, 132–36, 151, 154–55
planet, term, 130–31
planetarity, term, 132
Plath, Sylvia, 37
Plumwood, Val, 104, 115, 150
"Poem for Ireland, A," 161
poetry, 169–71
  and planetary poetics, 131–36
  and recovering grievable lives, 24–27
  birth of poets, 45
  charting shamanism in, 151–54
  class trauma allegory in, 20–24
  connections between myth, ritual, and, 125–26
  framing as magical speech, 152
  hybrid with scholarship, 12–15
  in public, 161–62
  "Life Isn't Going to Be the Same" (2020), 85–87
  magical state of mind in, 149–51
  of world being itself, 154–55
  patterning impulse in, 109–13
  poems as mirrors, 2–3
  poet as shape-shifter, 64–68
  quilt imagery in, 157–60
  reading bears in, 120–25
  reading bees in, 115–17
  resonance in, 5–6
  restoring communal role of, 22–23
  river metaphor describing, 128–30
  shamanic poet, 143–64
  spell poems in *Geomantic,* 155–57
  synesthesia in, 154–55
  "world" as term describing, 130–31
polar bears, reading. *See* bears, reading
Postcard from Iceland" (Heaney), 156
Postcolonial Ecocriticism (Huggan), 5
Precarious Life (Butler), 26–27
psychic skype, 162–63
public poem, 161–62
"Pyrolarty" *(Dharmakaya),* 39

quilt, imagery, 157–60
"Quilt, The" *(Geomantic)*, 158

Raleigh, Walter, 88
Randolph, Jody Allen, 2–3, 131, 151–52
re-enchantment, 8
Reading the Sky (Meehan), 55–60, 74–75, 79–80, 94–97, 129
recovery, grievable lives, 24–27
"Recovery" *(Dharmakaya),* 106–7
Reed, T. V., 50
Regarding Wave (Snyder), 74, 78–84
Reinventing Eden: The Fate of Nature in Western Culture (Merchant), 89
"Relishing the Conversation" (2020), 109–13
rescue, shedding illusion of, 103
residual, term, 66–67

Resnick, Stephen, 9
resonance, poetry and, 5–6
Return and No Blame (Meehan), 22–23, 93–94
 outside/inside dichotomy in, 53–55
River Moyne, 133–34
river, metaphors, 128–30
"Road to Agios Kirikos" *(Geomantic),* 164
Roediger, David, 9
romantic relationship, loss of context for, 97–99
Romanticism, 79
Rothenberg, Jerome, 153
Roy, Arundhati, 5

sacra, term, 60
sacredness, lack of, 38–42
Sands, Bobby. *See* "Hunger Strike" *(Reading the Sky)*
Saro-Wiwa, Ken, 5, 136
scholarship, poetry that is hybrid with, 12–15
science, between art and, 119
Scientific Revolution, 125, 147
"Scrying" *(Painting Rain),* 81–82, 147–48
Sea Cave, The" *(Geomantic),* 164
Seager, Joni, 60
Seeing Things (Heaney), 3
"Self on the Line, The" (2009), 12–19
 memoir-based pieces, 15–19
 poetry hybrid with scholarship, 12–15
self-definition, 35–37
Sered, Danielle, 64
Sexton, Anne, 25
shamanic poet
 and personal bee-loud glade, 163–64
 and public poem, 161–62
 and repressed Other of modernity, 144–46

synesthesia, 154–55
 earth magic, 155–57
 influence of Western magic on poetry, 143–44
 magical state of mind, 149–51
 reframing being human, 163–64
 shamanism and, 151–54
 witch as figure, 146–49
shamanism, 151–54
shape-shifting, 52
 in "Instructions to an Absent Husband," 55–60
 poet as shape-shifter, 64–68
 power of, 39–42
"She-Who-Walks-Among-The-People" *(Pillow Talk),* 20–24, 153, 105
Shenandoah, 1
Shiva, Vandana, 51, 75–76
Sidhe, 151–52
Sira, Ben, 102
Sivaraksa, Sulak, 29–30
"Six Sycamores" (Meehan), 80, 109
skyping, 162–63
Slow Violence and the Environmentalism of the Poor (Nixon), 5
Smith, R. T., 1
Snakey (character). See *Cell* (Meehan)
Snyder, Gary, 11–12, 52, 64, 66, 143, 152
 and "A Change of Life" sequence in *Painting Rain,* 78–84
 basic perception of animism, 75
 connecting work with ecopolitics, 75–77
 engagement with work of, 74–75
 entering generation of Meehan, 73–74
 guiding text made by, 134–36
 oeuvre of, 72–73
 shamanic role of, 125–26

socio-nature, 49–50
"Solace of Artemis, The" *(Imaginary Bonnets)*, 4, 114, 134, 151
    reading bears in, 121–25
    wedding of *mythos* and *technos* in, 126–28
"Solomon's Seal" *(Painting Rain)*, 81
"Song of Amergin" (Meehan), 152–52
"songs of the people," 88
Soto-Crespo, Ramóne, 89–90
"Southside Party" *(Return and No Blame)*, 54, 93–94
Spenser, Edmund, 88
Spillane, Allison, 49
spiritus mundi, "world soul" and, 144–45
Stanford, W. B., 86
"Statue of the Virgin at Granard Speaks, The" *(The Man Who Was Marked by Winter)*, 161
statues, giving voices to, 161–62
Steele, Cassie Premo, 24–25
Stevens, Maurice, 26
"Stink Bomb" *(Dharmakaya)*, 39
Straight-Creek-Great Basin" *(Turtle Island)*, 75
strategic animism, 76–77
street, reclaiming, 60–64
subsistence perspective, 51–52
"Sudden Rain" *(Dharmakaya)*, 38–39
"Swallows and Willows" *(Dharmakaya)*, 37
"Sweeping the Garden" *(Painting Rain)*, 81, 149
Synge, John, 128

"Tantric Master, The" *(Dharmakaya)*, 38
technos, wedding of *mythos* and, 126–28
"This Is Not a Confessional Poem" *(Painting Rain)*, 108

Thoreau, Henry David, 163
"Thunder in the House" *(Dharmakaya)*, 34–35
Thurman, Robert, 28
Tibetan Book of the Dead, The (Meehan), 23
    Buddhist perspective in, 28–30
Tiffin, Helen, 5
Tillinghast, Richard, 91
Time magazine, 120–21
To Penshurst (Johnson), 8
Toole, Christine, 165–66
trauma
    and recovering grievable lives, 24–27
    using term, 25–26
"Trauma is as Trauma Does" (Stevens), 26
trees, 73, 94, 135
    depiction in *The Golden Bough*, 77–78
    fulfilling role of kinship, 82–83
    granting status of "people of the land" to, 75
    mourning, 84
    women embracing, 76
    worshipping, 77–78
    writing about, 3–4
Tsing, Anna Lowenhaupt, 6
Turner, Victor, 60, 67–68
Turtle Island (Snyder), 75
20/12: Twenty Irish Poets Respond to Science in Twelve Lines, 119

U.S. Geological Survey, 121–22
Ulysses (Joyce), 170–71
Unclaimed Experience: Trauma, Narrative, and History (Caruth), 27
University College Dublin, 2–3
urban poetry, 8

"View from Under the Table, The" *(Dharmakaya)*, 32–33, 69
Villar-Argaíz, Pilar, 131
violence, recovering images of, 26–27
Virgin Mary, 161–62
vitalism, Neoplatonic magic and, 145–46
vocation, call of, 36–37

Waldau, Paul, 115
Walden (Thoreau), 163
War of Independence, 166
Warren, Karen, 50
We Heal from Memory (Steele), 24–25
West, academic training in, 13
West Indian writers, garden books of, 89–90
Western theories of magic
    overview, 143–44
    and repressed Other of modernity, 144–46
"What You Should Know to Be a Poet" *(Regarding Wave)*, 134–36. *See also* "Change of Life, A" *(Painting Rain)*
"When My Father Was a Young Man" *(Reading the Sky)*, 97
White, Lynn, Jr., 105
Whitehead, Ruth, 43

Williams, Raymond, 2, 8–9, 25, 36–37, 66–67, 98
witch
    figure, 146–49
    slur, 81–82
"Withdrawal, The" *(Geomantic)*, 164
Wolff, Richard, 9
women
    and Christian doctrine of Fall, 89
    and depiction of gardens in *Pillow Talk*, 99–108
    and witch as figure, 146–49
    Chipko beliefs, 76–77
    equating with animals, 57–59
    recasting female subject, 104–5
    reclaiming street, 60–64
women, disenfranchisement of, 53–54
Woolf, Virginia, 12
working class, topic, 8–10
world, term, 130–31
writer-activists, identifying, 5

Yanomami, tribe, 150–51, 155
Yeats, W. B., 128, 149

"Zugzwang" *(Man Who Was Marked by Winter, The)*, 97–99